Company's Coming®

Vegetarian

Easy & Delicious

Jean Paré

Front Cover

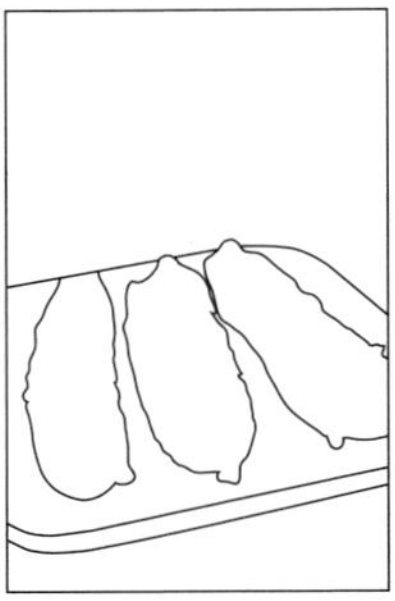

1. Stuffed Summer Squash, page 68

Back Cover

1. Veggie Rainbow Wraps, page 58
2. Western Portobello Burgers, page 56
3. Cheesy Chickpea Melt, page 62
4. Summer Mixed Grill, page 75
5. Grilled Stuffed Mushrooms, page 73
6. Vegetable Polenta Skewers, page 66

Printed in China

Library and Archives Canada Cataloguing in Publication

Paré, Jean, 1927-, author
Vegetarian : easy & delicious / Jean Paré.
(Original series)
Includes index.
Previously published: Edmonton, Alberta, Canada: Company's Coming Publishing Limited, 2013
ISBN 978-1-988133-30-0 (cerlox)
1. Vegetarian cooking. 2. Cookbooks. I. Title. II. Series: Paré, Jean, 1927- . Original series
TX837.P377 2017 641.5'636 C2016-905950-2

Distributed by
Canada Book Distributors – Booklogic
11414-119 Street
Edmonton. Alberta, Canada T5G 2X6
Tel: 1-800-661-9017

We acknowledge the financial support of the Government of Canada.

Funded by the Government of Canada
Financé par le gouvernement du Canada | Canada

PC: 28

We gratefully acknowledge the following suppliers for their generous support of our Test and Photography Kitchens:

Broil King Barbecues
Corelle®
Hamilton Beach® Canada
Lagostina®
Proctor Silex® Canada
Tupperware®

Company's Coming Cookbooks

Quick & easy recipes; everyday ingredients!

Original Series

- Softcover, 160 pages
- Lay-flat plastic comb binding
- Full-colour photos
- Nutrition information

Original Series

- Softcover, 160 pages
- Lay-flat plastic comb binding
- Full-colour photos
- Nutrition information

Original Series

- Softcover, 160 pages
- Lay-flat plastic comb binding
- Full-colour photos
- Nutrition information

Original Series

- Softcover, 160 pages
- Lay-flat plastic comb binding
- Full-colour photos
- Nutrition information

For a complete listing of our cookbooks, visit our website:

www.companyscoming.com

Table of Contents

Appetizers

Breakfasts & Brunches

Salads

Soups

Sandwiches, Burgers & Wraps

Mains

Sides

Snacks & Sweets

The Jean Paré Story

Jean Paré (pronounced "jeen PAIR-ee") grew up understanding that the combination of family, friends and home cooking is the best recipe for a good life. When Jean left home, she took with her a love of cooking, many family recipes and an intriguing desire to read cookbooks as if they were novels!

"Never share a recipe you wouldn't use yourself."

When her four children had all reached school age, Jean volunteered to cater the 50th anniversary celebration of the Vermilion School of Agriculture, now Lakeland College, in Alberta, Canada. Working from her home, Jean prepared a dinner for more than 1,000 people and from there launched a flourishing catering operation that continued for more than 18 years.

As requests for her recipes increased, Jean was often asked, "Why don't you write a cookbook?" The release of 150 Delicious Squares on April 14, 1981, marked the debut of what would soon turn into one of the world's most popular cookbook series.

Company's Coming cookbooks are distributed in Canada, the United States, Australia and other world markets. Bestsellers many times over in English, Company's Coming cookbooks have also been published in French and Spanish.

Familiar and trusted in home kitchens around the world, Company's Coming cookbooks are offered in a variety of formats. Highly regarded as kitchen workbooks, the softcover Original Series, with its lay-flat plastic comb binding, is still a favourite among home cooks.

Jean Paré's approach to cooking has always called for quick and easy recipes using everyday ingredients. That view served her well, and the tradition continues in the Practical Gourmet series.

Jean's Golden Rule of Cooking is: Never share a recipe you wouldn't use yourself. It's an approach that has worked—millions of times over!

Foreword

There are so many reasons today to eat vegetarian meals. Some people just don't care for meat or believe that, from a moral or environmental perspective, it isn't right to eat animal products. Others choose to incorporate a few vegetarian dishes into their weekly diets for health reasons. And others have simply discovered how refreshing, satisfying and delicious vegetarianism can be!

Eating a vegetarian diet has many benefits. Doctors and dietitians recommend going meatless for at least a couple of meals per week; Canada's Food Guide suggests having "meat alternatives such as beans, lentils and tofu often." And, of course, everyone knows that it's a good thing to eat more vegetables.

Not only do vegetarian options help you meet health goals like reducing fat and cholesterol in your diet, they can also be a more economical. Meat is often one of the most expensive ingredients, so reducing or eliminating it from your diet is a great way to save money.

A common challenge that people face when first starting to follow a vegetarian diet is meal planning. Because they are used to building their dishes around meat, many people are at a loss when it comes to preparing a meat-free meal. Others think that being a vegetarian means eating nothing but salad and tofu, and can't imagine how that can be filling. As the diverse and exciting selection of recipes in this cookbook proves, there is way more to eating vegetarian! With 126 recipes for all types of dishes, from brunches to snacks to main courses, Vegetarian will help you make delicious, satisfying, tried-and-true vegetarian meals.

Serve our eye-catching Sushi Vegetable Squares as an appetizer, then follow it up with the truly tremendous Vegan Pad Thai, or the Lasagna Fagiole that's been bubbling away in the slow cooker all afternoon. Avocado Quinoa Salad is oh-so satisfying and refreshing (and pretty!), and our decadent Chocolate Tofu Cake will win over even tofu skeptics. You'll discover very quickly that there are many delicious ways to eat vegetarian.

We've included a number of vegan recipes in this book, which are indicated by icons. And among this collection of modern vegetarian dishes, we've also included a handful of Company's Coming Classics that have stood the test of time. Whether you're a brand new vegetarian or an experienced veteran, a vegan or just someone who wants to eat a bit less meat, you'll find much to love in Vegetarian!

Nutrition Information Guidelines

Each recipe is analyzed using the most current versions of the Canadian Nutrient File from Health Canada, and the United States Department of Agriculture (USDA) Nutrient Database for Standard Reference.

- If more than one ingredient is listed (such as "butter or hard margarine"), or if a range is given (1 – 2 tsp., 5 – 10 mL), only the first ingredient or first amount is analyzed.
- Milk used is 1% M.F. (milk fat), unless otherwise stated.
- Cooking oil used is canola oil, unless otherwise stated.
- Ingredients indicating "sprinkle," "optional" or "for garnish" are not included in the nutrition information.
- The fat in recipes and combination foods can vary greatly depending upon the sources and types of fats used in each specific ingredient. For these reasons, the amount of saturated, monounsaturated and polyunsaturated fats may not add up to the total fat content.

Introduction

Vegetarianism has been common in Asia for thousands of years, and it has steadily grown in popularity in North America for decades. No longer considered a fringe lifestyle in the West, vegetarianism is now main stream, and vegetarian options abound in restaurants, grocery stores and even fast food chains. Whether the choice to eat vegetarian food is dictated by personal preference, dietary concerns, religion or culture, vegetarianism is part of a healthy lifestyle.

What Is a Vegetarian?

The obvious answer is "a person who does not eat meat," but in truth it is not quite that simple. Among varying degrees of vegetarianism are people who choose not to eat mammals but still consider fish and poultry fair game; others do not consume the meat of any animal but still eat milk products or eggs. On the stricter end of the spectrum, vegans do not allow for the consumption or use of any animal products or by-products, including dairy, honey and gelatine as well as non-food items such as silk, wool and leather. A more recent addition to the vegetarian family is the so-called flexitarian—someone who follows a mostly vegetarian diet but still eats meat on occasion.

WHY VEGETARIAN?

There are many reasons why someone might choose a vegetarian diet, one of which is cost. Meat is one of the most expensive foods, and for millions of people worldwide it is too expensive to eat on a regular basis, if at all. Reducing or cutting meat from your diet can help lower your grocery bill.

Environmental concerns are another reason some people choose to not eat meat. The meat industry consumes a large amount of natural resources, whereas the production of plant protein uses far less water and fossil fuels. Many environmental organizations have claimed that the meat industry, in its current state, is not sustainable and contributes to climate change and world hunger.

For some people, animal rights play a role in their choice to adopt a vegetarian diet.

Most people who eat vegetarian food, however, do so for the health benefits. It was once thought that a vegetarian diet couldn't possibly be healthy but the reverse, in fact, is true. Vegetarian diets are high in fruits and vegetables, whole grains, nuts and seeds, all of which promote good health. They are also generally low saturated fat and cholesterol, and high in fibre (and most of us don't eat enough of that).

What About Protein?

A common myth about vegetarianism is that it is impossible to get enough protein without eating meat. Not true. Many plant foods are also excellent sources of protein. The difference is that animal proteins are "complete proteins," meaning that they contain all the essential amino acids (those that the body cannot produce and must get from external sources). Proteins derived from fruits, vegetables, nuts and grains, however, are "incomplete proteins" because they do not contain all the essential amino acids (with the exception of quinoa and soybeans). It was once thought that to get complete protein from a vegetarian diet, certain foods had to be paired in the same meal. Research has shown that is not the case. There is no complicated formula you must follow; by simply eating a variety of foods from the different plant groups throughout the day, you'll get all the essential animo acids your body needs.

VEGETARIAN PROTEIN SOURCES

Whole grains—grains have been given a bad rap lately as low-carb diets have gained in popularity, but whole grains are a great source of protein as well as carbohydrates, and they definitely have a place in a healthy diet. The trick is to choose grains that still have all three parts of the kernel, such as rolled oats and brown rice, instead of highly refined grains, such as all-purpose flour and white rice.

Legumes—beans and lentils are excellent sources of protein, and they are low in fat and high in fibre. They are also one of the least expensive protein sources available. Black beans, chickpeas, kidney beans, cannellini beans, green lentils, red lentils, the list goes on and on. With so many choices, you'll never get tired of eating legumes.

Soy—soy products have been flooding the market in the past few years, and although soy can be a healthy addition to your diet, again you want to stay away from the highly processed versions. Tofu (also called soybean curd) and miso (a paste made from fermented soybeans) are the best soy options to choose for their nutritional value and protein content.

Dairy—not only are dairy products a source of complete protein, they are also high in calcium, a mineral essential to good health. Many people do not get enough calcium.

Eggs—eggs are another source of complete protein and are very rich in nutrients, but they are also high in fat and cholesterol.

Essential Vegetarian Ingredients

Cheese (ricotta, Cheddar, mozzarella, Parmesan)

Coconut milk

Dried fruits (cranberries, apricots, dates, raisins)

Edamame (shelled)

Fruit (apples, banana, oranges, lemon, limes, frozen mango, frozen mixed berries, canned peaches, canned pears)

Grains (pearl and pot barley, bulgur, quinoa, couscous)

Legumes, both dried and canned (chickpeas, kidney, white, black)

Lentils (red, green, canned)

Milk (regular, soy, rice)

Nuts (almonds, cashews, pine nuts, pecans)

Nut butters (almond, peanut)

Pasta and noodles (any short or long pasta; egg, soba, rice noodles)

Rice (brown, wild, white)

Seeds (sesame, sunflower, pumpkin)

Tofu (firm, medium, silken)

Vegetable broth

Vegetables, frozen (peas, corn, mixed, spinach)

Vegetables, fresh (a variety—onion, garlic, bell peppers, carrot, celery, lettuce, English cucumber, tomatoes, potatoes, mushrooms)

Yogurt (plain)

Layered Middle Eastern Dip

Nice contrasting flavours and textures with creamy yogurt, lentils and a smooth red pepper purée topped with a sprinkle of toasted pine nuts, crisp cucumber and tomato. Serve this layered dip with crackers, pita breads or pita chips.

Jar of roasted red peppers, drained	**12 oz.**	**340 mL**
Walnut pieces	**3/4 cup**	**175 mL**
Fine dry bread crumbs	**1/4 cup**	**60 mL**
Olive (or cooking) oil	**2 tbsp.**	**30 mL**
Garlic clove, minced (or 1/4 tsp., 1 mL, powder)	**1**	**1**
Paprika	**1 tsp.**	**5 mL**
Liquid honey	**1/2 tsp.**	**2 mL**
Envelope of onion soup mix (stir before dividing)	**1 1/4 oz.**	**38 g**
Can of lentils, rinsed and drained	**19 oz.**	**540 mL**
Plain Balkan-style yogurt	**1 1/2 cups**	**375 mL**
Chopped fresh parsley (or 1 1/2 tsp., 7 mL, flakes)	**2 tbsp.**	**30 mL**
Lemon juice	**2 tbsp.**	**30 mL**
Ground cumin	**1/2 tsp.**	**2 mL**
Chopped English cucumber (with peel)	**1/2 cup**	**125 mL**
Chopped seeded tomato	**1/2 cup**	**125 mL**
Pine nuts, toasted (see Tip, page 148)	**1/4 cup**	**60 mL**

Process first 7 ingredients and half of soup mix in blender or food processor until smooth. Spread in ungreased 8 x 8 inch (20 x 20 cm) baking dish.

Combine next 5 ingredients and remaining soup mix in small bowl. Spread over red pepper mixture. Chill for 2 hours.

Scatter remaining 3 ingredients over top. Makes about 6 1/2 cups (1.6 L).

1/4 cup (60 mL): *80 Calories; 5 g Total Fat (1.5 g Mono, 2.5 g Poly, 0.5 g Sat); 0 mg Cholesterol; 7 g Carbohydrate; 1 g Fibre; 3 g Protein; 170 mg Sodium*

Caponata

Our take on caponata *is packed with eggplant and veggies. Serve chilled or at room temperature with whole-grain crackers or whole-wheat pita bread. Freeze leftovers in an airtight container for up to three months.*

Chopped peeled eggplant (1 1/2 inch, 4 cm, pieces)	**5 cups**	**1.25 L**
Olive oil	**1 tbsp.**	**15 mL**
Chopped onion	**1 cup**	**250 mL**
Finely chopped celery	**1 cup**	**250 mL**
Garlic cloves, minced	**2**	**2**
Dried crushed chilies	**1/4 tsp.**	**1 mL**
Can of diced tomatoes (with juice)	**14 oz.**	**398 mL**
Diced red pepper	**1 cup**	**250 mL**
Diced zucchini (with peel)	**1 cup**	**250 mL**
Balsamic vinegar	**2 tbsp.**	**30 mL**
Tomato paste	**1 tbsp.**	**15 mL**
Granulated sugar	**2 tsp.**	**10 mL**
Dried oregano	**1 1/2 tsp.**	**7 mL**
Sliced black olives, chopped	**1/3 cup**	**75 mL**
Chopped capers (optional)	**2 tsp.**	**10 mL**
Chopped fresh basil	**1 tbsp.**	**15 mL**
Chopped pine nuts, toasted (see Tip, page 148)	**1 tbsp.**	**15 mL**

Arrange eggplant in single layer on greased baking sheet. Broil on top rack in oven for about 5 minutes, stirring occasionally, until browned and starting to soften. Transfer to greased 3 1/2 to 4 quart (3.5 to 4 L) slow cooker.

Heat olive oil in large frying pan on medium. Add onion and celery. Cook for about 8 minutes, stirring often, until onion starts to soften. Add garlic and chilies. Heat and stir for about 1 minute until fragrant. Add to slow cooker.

Add next 7 ingredients. Stir. Cook, covered, on Low for 5 to 6 hours or on High for 2 1/2 to 3 hours. Transfer to large bowl.

Add olives and capers. Stir. Cool. Chill, covered, for at least 6 hours.

Sprinkle with basil and pine nuts. Makes about 4 1/2 cups (1.1 L).

1/4 cup (60 mL): *35 Calories; 1.5 g Total Fat (1 g Mono, 0 g Poly, 0 g Sat); 0 mg Cholesterol; 6 g Carbohydrate; 2 g Fibre; trace Protein; 110 mg Sodium*

Artichoke Pine Nut Spread

A creamy and light dip. Serve with sliced carrots and zucchini or with whole-grain crackers.

Cans of artichoke hearts (14 oz., 398 mL, each), drained	**2**	**2**
Pine nuts, toasted (see Tip, page 148)	**1/2 cup**	**125 mL**
Olive oil	**2 tbsp.**	**30 mL**
Italian seasoning	**1 1/2 tsp.**	**7 mL**
Salt	**1/4 tsp.**	**1 mL**

Process all 5 ingredients in blender or food processor until almost smooth. Makes about 2 cups (500 mL).

1/4 cup (60 mL): *110 Calories; 10 g Total Fat (4 g Mono, 3.5 g Poly, 1 g Sat); 0 mg Cholesterol; 4 g Carbohydrate; 2 g Fibre; 2 g Protein; 270 mg Sodium*

Curry Spiced Vegetable Triangles

Crispy, flaky triangles enclose a delicious curried potato filling. You can prepare these in advance and then freeze them, uncooked, and bake them later.

Olive oil	**1 tsp.**	**5 mL**
Chopped onion	**1 1/2 cups**	**375 mL**
Hot curry paste	**1 tbsp.**	**15 mL**
Finely grated ginger root (or 1/4 tsp., 1 mL, ground ginger)	**1 tsp.**	**5 mL**
Garlic cloves, minced (or 1/2 tsp., 2 mL, powder)	**2**	**2**
Diced peeled potato	**1 1/2 cups**	**375 mL**
Prepared vegetable broth	**3/4 cup**	**175 mL**
Salt	**1/4 tsp.**	**1 mL**
Frozen peas	**1/3 cup**	**75 mL**
Lemon juice	**1 tsp.**	**5 mL**

(continued on next page)

Phyllo pastry sheets, thawed according to package directions	**12**	**12**
Olive oil	**1/4 cup**	**60 mL**

Ground cumin, sprinkle
Paprika, sprinkle

Heat olive oil in large frying pan on medium. Add onion. Cook for about 10 minutes, stirring often, until onion is softened.

Add next 3 ingredients. Heat and stir for about 1 minute until fragrant.

Add next 3 ingredients. Stir. Bring to a boil. Reduce heat to medium-low. Simmer, covered, for about 20 minutes, stirring occasionally, until potato is tender.

Add peas and lemon juice. Heat and stir for 1 minute. Transfer to medium bowl. Cool.

Place 1 pastry sheet on work surface. Cover remaining sheets with damp towel to prevent drying. Brush sheet with olive oil. Place second pastry sheet over top. Brush with olive oil. Cut lengthwise into 4 strips. Spoon about 1 tbsp. (15 mL) potato mixture onto bottom of strip. Fold 1 corner diagonally towards straight edge to form triangle. Continue folding back and forth, enclosing filling (see Diagram). Repeat with remaining pastry sheets, olive oil and potato mixture. Arrange on greased baking sheets (see Note). Brush with remaining olive oil.

Sprinkle with cumin and paprika. Bake in 375°F (190°C) oven for about 15 minutes until golden. Makes 24 triangles.

1 triangle: *80 Calories; 3 g Total Fat (2 g Mono, 0 g Poly, 0 g Sat); 0 mg Cholesterol; 11 g Carbohydrate; trace Fibre; 2 g Protein; 125 mg Sodium*

Note: Triangles can be frozen uncooked. Brush frozen triangles with olive oil. Bake in 375°F (190°C) oven for about 18 to 20 minutes until golden and heated through.

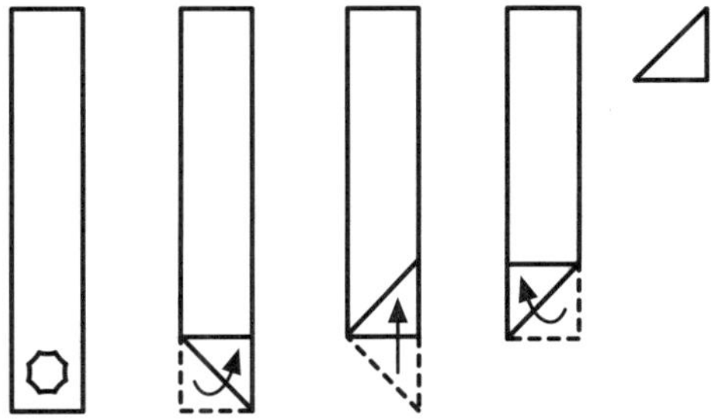

Mushroom Salad Rolls

A filling of mushrooms, bamboo shoots and Thai condiments wrapped in rice paper. Rice paper rounds are available in the Asian section of grocery stores or in specialty Asian stores. If you cannot find shiitake or oyster mushrooms, substitute equal amounts of brown mushrooms.

Cooking oil	**1 tsp.**	**5 mL**
Thinly sliced fresh shiitake mushrooms	**1 cup**	**250 mL**
Thinly sliced fresh oyster mushrooms	**1 cup**	**250 mL**
Canned shoestring-style bamboo shoots, drained	**1/2 cup**	**125 mL**
Finely chopped onion	**1/4 cup**	**60 mL**
Sliced green onion	**1/4 cup**	**60 mL**
Finely grated ginger root (or 1/2 tsp., 2 mL, ground ginger)	**2 tsp.**	**10 mL**
Garlic clove, minced (or 1/4 tsp., 1 mL, powder)	**1**	**1**
Hoisin sauce	**2 tbsp.**	**30 mL**
Lime juice	**1 tbsp.**	**15 mL**
Soy sauce	**1 tbsp.**	**15 mL**
Chili paste (sambal oelek)	**1/2 tsp.**	**2 mL**
Rice paper rounds (6 inch, 15 cm, diameter)	**6**	**6**
Small butter lettuce leaves	**6**	**6**

Heat cooking oil in large frying pan on medium. Add next 7 ingredients. Cook for about 5 minutes, stirring occasionally, until mushrooms release their liquid.

Add next 4 ingredients. Heat and stir for 1 minute. Remove from heat. Let stand for 10 minutes.

Place 1 rice paper round in pie plate or shallow bowl of hot water until just softened. Place on work surface. Place 1 lettuce leaf on round. Spoon about 1/4 cup (60 mL) mushroom mixture over lettuce. Fold sides over filling. Roll up tightly from bottom to enclose filling. Place on plate. Cover with damp paper towel. Repeat with remaining rounds, lettuce and mushroom mixture. Makes 6 rolls.

1 roll: *35 Calories; 1 g Total Fat (0.5 g Mono, 0 g Poly, 0 g Sat); 0 mg Cholesterol; 5 g Carbohydrate; trace Fibre; 2 g Protein; 250 mg Sodium*

Pictured on page 36.

Sushi Vegetable Squares

We skipped soy sauce to make this easy version of sushi gluten-free. Put a layer of plastic wrap over the rice so you can press it evenly into the pan without the rice sticking to your hands.

Water	2 1/4 cups	550 mL
Short-grain white rice, rinsed and drained	1 1/2 cups	375 mL
Rice vinegar	3 tbsp.	45 mL
Granulated sugar	2 tbsp.	30 mL
Dried crushed chilies	1 tsp.	5 mL
Salt	1/2 tsp.	2 mL
Diced roasted red pepper	1/2 cup	125 mL
Grated carrot	1/2 cup	125 mL
Salted, roasted sunflower seeds	1/4 cup	60 mL
Mayonnaise	2 tbsp.	30 mL
Dijon mustard	1 tsp.	5 mL
Large avocado, thinly sliced	1	1
Cherry tomato slices	16	16
Finely chopped fresh chives	1 tbsp.	15 mL

Pour water into small saucepan. Bring to a boil. Add rice. Stir. Reduce heat to medium-low. Simmer, covered, for 20 minutes without stirring. Remove from heat. Let stand, covered, for 10 minutes, until rice is tender and liquid is absorbed. Transfer to large bowl.

Stir next 4 ingredients in small bowl until sugar is dissolved. Add to rice. Stir. Let stand until cool.

Line bottom of 9 x 9 inch (23 x 23 cm) pan with foil, leaving 1 inch (2.5 cm) overhang on 2 sides. Press half of rice mixture firmly into pan. Toss next 5 ingredients in medium bowl. Spread over rice. Arrange avocado over top. Press remaining rice mixture evenly over avocado. Chill, covered, for 1 hour. Holding foil, remove from pan. Using wet knife, cut into 16 squares. Arrange squares on serving plate.

Garnish with tomato and chives. Makes 16 squares.

1 square: *130 Calories; 4 g Total Fat (0.5 g Mono, 1 g Poly, 1.5 g Sat); 0 mg Cholesterol; 20 g Carbohydrate; 2 g Fibre; 2 g Protein; 110 mg Sodium*

Pictured on page 72.

Root Vegetable Tapenade

The sweet earthy flavours of roasted root vegetables are enhanced with balsamic vinegar and blue cheese. If you are not a blue cheese fan, substitute shaved Parmesan or soft goat (chèvre) cheese. To make this vegan, omit cheese. Serve warm or cold with gluten-free crackers

Fresh medium beet (about 8 oz., 225 g), scrubbed clean and trimmed	**1**	**1**
Small fennel bulb (about 7 oz., 200 g), halved	**1**	**1**
Small onion (about 6 oz., 170 g), halved	**1**	**1**
Crumbled blue cheese (optional)	**2 tbsp.**	**30 mL**
Chopped fresh chives	**1 tbsp.**	**15 mL**
Olive (or cooking) oil	**1 tbsp.**	**15 mL**
Balsamic vinegar	**1 tbsp.**	**15 mL**
Salt	**1/8 tsp.**	**0.5 mL**
Pepper, sprinkle		
Chopped fresh chives	**1 tsp.**	**5 mL**

Wrap beet, fennel and onion individually with foil. Bake on foil-lined baking sheet with sides in 375°F (190°C) oven for about 1 hour until tender. Discard foil. Let stand for about 5 minutes until cool enough to handle. Peel and chop beet. Chop fennel and onion. Transfer to food processor.

Add next 6 ingredients. Process using on/off motion until vegetables are coarsely chopped.

Sprinkle with second amount of chives. Makes about 2 cups (500 mL).

1/4 cup (60 mL): *50 Calories; 2.5 g Total Fat (1.5 g Mono, 0 g Poly, 0.5 g Sat); 0 mg Cholesterol; 7 g Carbohydrate; 2 g Fibre; 1 g Protein; 100 mg Sodium*

Pictured on page 36.

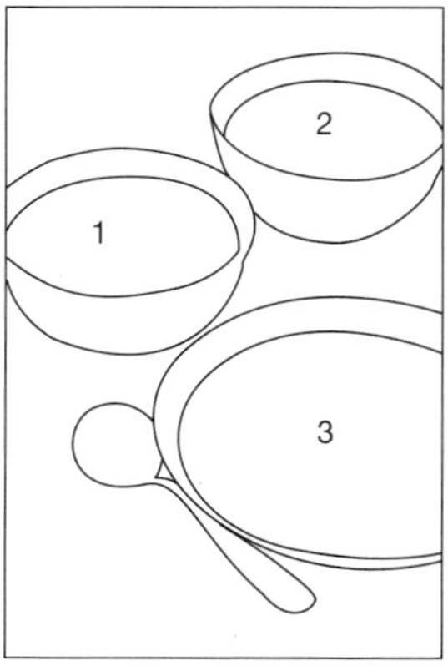

1. Edamame Pepper Soup, page 42
2. Swiss Chard Soup, page 49
3. Tomato Lentil Soup, page 50

Salsa-stuffed Avocados

VEGAN

Leave the skin intact on the avocados when you halve them and scoop out the flesh. The shells, once refilled, serve as a dish; all you need is a spoon to enjoy!

Chopped seeded tomato	**1 cup**	**250 mL**
Diced yellow pepper	**1/2 cup**	**125 mL**
Frozen kernel corn, thawed	**1/4 cup**	**60 mL**
Chopped fresh cilantro (or parsley)	**2 tbsp.**	**30 mL**
Finely chopped red onion	**2 tbsp.**	**30 mL**
Lime juice	**2 tbsp.**	**30 mL**
Olive oil	**1 tbsp.**	**15 mL**
Salt	**1/8 tsp.**	**0.5 mL**
Pepper	**1/8 tsp.**	**0.5 mL**
Small avocados, halved	**2**	**2**

Combine first 9 ingredients in medium bowl.

Using a spoon, remove avocado flesh. Reserve shells. Dice avocado flesh. Add to tomato mixture. Stir. Spoon into shells. Makes 4 stuffed avocado halves.

1 stuffed avocado half: *210 Calories; 17 g Total Fat (11 g Mono, 2 g Poly, 2.5 g Sat); 0 mg Cholesterol; 15 g Carbohydrate; 8 g Fibre; 4 g Protein; 105 mg Sodium*

Pictured on page 36.

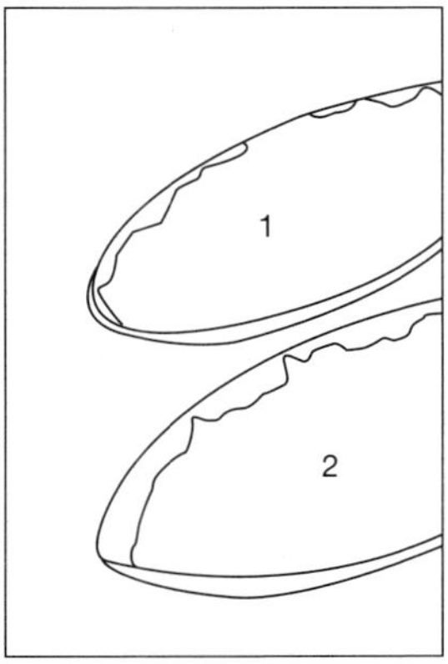

1. Hazelnut Squash Penne, page 120
2. Butternut Pesto Risotto, page 128

Artichoke Pinwheels

Tasty spiralled biscuits with a rich artichoke and three-cheese filling. These elegant biscuits are perfect for a special occasion brunch.

Jar of marinated artichoke hearts, drained, blotted dry, finely chopped	**6 oz.**	**170 mL**
Grated sharp Cheddar cheese	**1/2 cup**	**125 mL**
Crumbled feta cheese	**1/4 cup**	**60 mL**
Finely chopped green onion	**1/4 cup**	**60 mL**
Grated Parmesan cheese	**2 tbsp.**	**30 mL**
All-purpose flour	**2 cups**	**500 mL**
Baking powder	**4 tsp.**	**20 mL**
Dried dillweed	**1 tsp.**	**5 mL**
Salt	**1/2 tsp.**	**2 mL**
Cold butter (or hard margarine), cut up	**1/4 cup**	**60 mL**
Milk	**3/4 cup**	**175 mL**
Milk	**1 tbsp.**	**15 mL**

Combine first 5 ingredients in small bowl.

Combine next 4 ingredients in large bowl. Cut in butter until mixture resembles coarse crumbs. Make a well in centre. Add first amount of milk to well. Stir until soft dough forms. Turn out onto lightly floured surface. Knead 8 times. Roll or pat out to 8 x 12 inch (20 x 30 cm) rectangle. Spread artichoke mixture evenly over dough, leaving 1 inch (2.5 cm) edge on 1 long side. Roll up, jelly-roll style, from covered long side. Press seam against roll to seal. Cut into 12 slices. Arrange, cut-side up, about 1 inch (2.5 cm) apart on parchment paper–lined baking sheet.

Brush with second amount of milk. Bake in 375°F (190°C) oven for about 23 minutes until golden. Let stand on baking sheet for 5 minutes before removing to wire rack to cool. Makes 12 pinwheels.

***1 pinwheel:** 160 Calories; 7 g Total Fat (1.5 g Mono, 0 g Poly, 4.5 g Sat); 20 mg Cholesterol; 18 g Carbohydrate; trace Fibre; 5 g Protein; 350 mg Sodium*

Ricotta Spinach Bake

Tender macaroni is paired with rich ricotta and nutritious spinach. A filling brunch option.

Elbow macaroni	**1 1/2 cups**	**375 mL**
Chopped fresh spinach leaves, lightly packed	**2 cups**	**500 mL**
Ricotta cheese	**2 cups**	**500 mL**
Grated Asiago cheese	**2/3 cup**	**150 mL**
All-purpose flour	**1/4 cup**	**60 mL**
Basil pesto	**1 tbsp.**	**15 mL**
Grated lemon zest	**1/4 tsp.**	**1 mL**
Pepper	**1/4 tsp.**	**1 mL**

Cook pasta according to package directions. Drain.

Combine remaining 7 ingredients in large bowl. Add pasta. Stir. Spread evenly in greased 8 x 8 inch (20 x 20 cm) baking dish. Bake, covered, in 375°F (190°C) oven for 20 minutes. Remove cover. Bake for about 15 minutes until edges are golden. Let stand for 10 minutes. Cuts into 6 pieces.

1 piece: *310 Calories; 11 g Total Fat (2 g Mono, 0 g Poly, 6 g Sat); 35 mg Cholesterol; 35 g Carbohydrate; 2 g Fibre; 17 g Protein; 220 mg Sodium*

Caramelized Leek Quiche

Caramelizing the leeks gives this quiche a slight sweetness, while the goat cheese provides a complementary tang.

Pastry for 9 inch (23 cm) deep dish pie shell	**1**	**1**
Cooking oil	**2 tbsp.**	**30 mL**
Sliced leek (white part only)	**3 cups**	**750 mL**
Large eggs, fork-beaten	**4**	**4**
Half-and-half cream	**1 cup**	**250 mL**
Dijon mustard	**2 tsp.**	**10 mL**
Dried thyme	**1/2 tsp.**	**2 mL**
Salt	**1/2 tsp.**	**2 mL**
Pepper	**1/4 tsp.**	**1 mL**
Goat (chèvre) cheese, cut up	**4 oz.**	**113 g**
Grated Swiss cheese	**3/4 cup**	**175 mL**

Roll out pastry on lightly floured surface to 1/8 inch (3 mm) thickness. Line 9 inch (23 cm) deep dish pie plate with pastry. Trim, leaving 1/2 inch (12 mm) overhang. Roll under and crimp decorative edge.

Heat cooking oil in large frying pan on medium. Add leeks. Cook for about 15 minutes, stirring occasionally, until softened and browned. Remove from heat. Let stand for 5 minutes to cool slightly. Spread evenly in pie shell.

Whisk next 6 ingredients in large bowl. Pour into pie shell.

Scatter goat cheese and Swiss cheese over top. Bake on bottom rack in 375°F (190°C) oven for about 50 minutes until knife inserted in centre of quiche comes out clean. Let stand for 10 minutes. Cuts into 6 wedges.

1 wedge: *430 Calories; 32 g Total Fat (13 g Mono, 5 g Poly, 12 g Sat); 125 mg Cholesterol; 22 g Carbohydrate; 2 g Fibre; 13 g Protein; 560 mg Sodium*

Tex-Mex Tofu Scramble

The bold flavours of this hearty breakfast will awaken your taste buds. Wrap a tortilla around it, and you have breakfast-on-the-go.

Olive oil	**1 tbsp.**	**15 mL**
Chopped onion	**1/2 cup**	**125 mL**
Package of firm tofu, drained and crumbled	**12.75 oz.**	**350 g**
Chopped red pepper	**2/3 cup**	**150 mL**
Frozen kernel corn, thawed	**2/3 cup**	**150 mL**
Chili powder	**1 tsp.**	**5 mL**
Salt	**1/4 tsp.**	**1 mL**
Pepper	**1/8 tsp.**	**0.5 mL**
Salsa	**3/4 cup**	**175 mL**
Chopped fresh cilantro (or parsley)	**2 tbsp.**	**30 mL**

Heat olive oil in large frying pan on medium. Add onion. Cook for about 5 minutes, stirring often, until softened.

Add next 6 ingredients. Scramble-fry for about 12 minutes until tofu is browned and hot.

Add salsa. Stir until heated through. Remove from heat.

Add cilantro. Stir gently. Makes about 3 cups (750 mL).

3/4 cup (175 mL): *210 Calories; 10 g Total Fat (2.5 g Mono, 0 g Poly, 2 g Sat); 0 mg Cholesterol; 16 g Carbohydrate; 4 g Fibre; 14 g Protein; 570 mg Sodium*

Mango Almond Smoothie

Super simple and full of protein. Frozen fruit adds a creamy element to this power-packed smoothie.

Frozen mango pieces	**3 cups**	**750 mL**
Vanilla soy milk, chilled	**2 cups**	**500 mL**
Can of sliced peaches (in juice)	**14 oz.**	**398 mL**
Almond butter	**1/4 cup**	**60 mL**

Process all 4 ingredients in blender or food processor until smooth. Makes about 6 cups (1.5 L).

1 cup (250 mL): *170 Calories; 7 g Total Fat (0 g Mono, 0.5 g Poly, 0.5 g Sat); 0 mg Cholesterol; 23 g Carbohydrate; 3 g Fibre; 5 g Protein; 45 mg Sodium*

Pictured on page 108.

Smoky Mushroom Frittata

A colourful frittata that's pretty to look at and filled with satisfying tastes that will please almost anyone. We've omitted the flour or baking mix added to many egg dishes to make this frittata gluten-free. Garnish with extra cherry tomatoes if desired.

Cooking oil	**1 tsp.**	**5 mL**
Sliced fresh white mushrooms	**2 cups**	**500 mL**
Chopped onion	**1 cup**	**250 mL**
Chopped red pepper	**1 cup**	**250 mL**
Chopped green onion	**1/2 cup**	**125 mL**
Large eggs	**12**	**12**
Milk	**1/4 cup**	**60 mL**
Salt	**1/2 tsp.**	**2 mL**
Pepper	**1/4 tsp.**	**1 mL**
Grated smoked Cheddar cheese	**1 cup**	**250 mL**
Quartered cherry tomatoes	**1 cup**	**250 mL**
Chopped fresh basil	**2 tbsp.**	**30 mL**

Heat cooking oil in large non-stick frying pan on medium. Add mushrooms and onion. Cook for about 10 minutes, stirring occasionally, until mushrooms start to brown.

Add red pepper and green onion. Cook for about 2 minutes, stirring occasionally, until red pepper is softened.

Whisk next 4 ingredients in medium bowl. Pour over vegetables. Stir. Reduce heat to medium-low. Cook, covered, for about 18 minutes until bottom is golden and top is set. Remove from heat.

Sprinkle with cheese. Let stand, covered, for about 2 minutes until cheese is melted.

Scatter tomato and basil over top. Cuts into 6 wedges.

1 wedge: *180 Calories; 11 g Total Fat (3.5 g Mono, 1.5 g Poly, 4 g Sat); 280 mg Cholesterol; 13 g Carbohydrate; 2 g Fibre; 13 g Protein; 340 mg Sodium*

Pictured on page 108.

Apple Pumpkin Pie Toast

Kids will love this baked French toast with pumpkin pie flavours and a fruity topping. Use two- or three-day-old bread for best results. Drizzle with maple syrup, if desired.

Vanilla soy (or rice) milk	**1 cup**	**250 mL**
Canned pure pumpkin (no spices), see Tip, below	**3/4 cup**	**175 mL**
Maple syrup	**1/4 cup**	**60 mL**
Ground cinnamon	**1/2 tsp.**	**2 mL**
Ground ginger	**1/4 tsp.**	**1 mL**
Ground cloves, just a pinch		
French bread slices (cut 3/4 inch, 2 cm, thick)	**8**	**8**
Can of apple pie filling	**19 oz.**	**540 mL**
Chopped fresh (or frozen, thawed) cranberries	**1/2 cup**	**125 mL**

Whisk first 6 ingredients in large bowl until smooth.

Dip bread slices into pumpkin mixture. Arrange in single layer in well-greased baking sheet. Pour any remaining pumpkin mixture over top. Bake on bottom rack in 375°F (190°C) oven for about 15 minutes until bottom is browned. Turn.

Combine pie filling and cranberries in medium bowl. Spoon over bread. Bake for about 15 minutes until bottom is browned. Let stand for 5 minutes. Makes 8 toasts.

__1 toast:__ 170 Calories; 1 g Total Fat (0 g Mono, 0 g Poly, 0 g Sat); 0 mg Cholesterol; 38 g Carbohydrate; 4 g Fibre; 3 g Protein; 160 mg Sodium

Pictured on page 108.

tip Be careful to purchase the right type of canned pumpkin that your recipe calls for. Pure pumpkin is just that—pumpkin with nothing added. Pumpkin pie filling, on the other hand, is pumpkin that has been blended with sugar and spices.

Banana Maple Pecan Pancakes

Bits of banana and pecans dress up your Saturday morning pancakes! Serve with extra maple syrup.

All-purpose flour	**2 cups**	**500 mL**
Chopped pecans, toasted (see Tip, page 148)	**1/2 cup**	**125 mL**
Baking powder	**1 tbsp.**	**15 mL**
Ground cinnamon	**1/4 tsp.**	**1 mL**
Salt	**1/4 tsp.**	**1 mL**
Diced overripe banana	**1 1/2 cups**	**375 mL**
Soy (or rice) milk	**1 3/4 cups**	**425 mL**
Maple syrup	**1/4 cup**	**60 mL**
Cooking oil	**2 tbsp.**	**30 mL**

Combine first 5 ingredients in large bowl. Make a well in centre.

Mash half of banana in medium bowl. Add remaining 3 ingredients. Mix until smooth. Stir in remaining banana. Add to well. Stir until just combined. Batter will be lumpy. Preheat electric griddle to medium-high (see Note). Spray griddle with cooking spray. Pour batter onto griddle, using 1/4 cup (60 mL) for each pancake. Cook for about 3 minutes until bubbles form on top and edges appear dry. Turn pancake over. Cook for about 2 minutes until bottom is golden. Transfer to plate. Cover to keep warm. Repeat with remaining batter, spraying griddle with more cooking spray if necessary to prevent sticking. Makes about 15 pancakes.

***1 pancake:** 140 Calories; 5 g Total Fat (3 g Mono, 1.5 g Poly, 0 g Sat); 0 mg Cholesterol; 22 g Carbohydrate; 1 g Fibre; 3 g Protein; 110 mg Sodium*

Note: If you don't have an electric griddle, use a large frying pan. Replace cooking spray with 1 tsp. (5 mL) cooking oil and heat on medium. Heat more cooking oil with each batch if necessary to prevent sticking.

Piña Colada Brunch Bake

Rich and satisfying, a little of this decadent dish goes a long way! To make this kid-friendly, don't drain the can of pineapple and omit the rum. Pair with a medley of fresh tropical fruit.

Can of crushed pineapple, drained	**14 oz.**	**398 mL**
Golden raisins	**1/2 cup**	**125 mL**
Amber (golden) rum	**1/3 cup**	**75 mL**
Cubed baguette	**5 cups**	**1.25 L**
Can of coconut milk	**14 oz.**	**398 mL**
Brown sugar, packed	**1/4 cup**	**60 mL**
Ground cinnamon	**1/2 tsp.**	**2 mL**
Ground allspice	**1/4 tsp.**	**1 mL**
Medium sweetened coconut, toasted (see Tip, page 148)	**1/2 cup**	**125 mL**

Combine first 3 ingredients in small bowl. Let stand for 10 minutes.

Arrange bread cubes in single layer on ungreased baking sheet with sides. Bake in 350°F (175°C) oven for about 15 minutes, stirring at halftime, until toasted.

Stir next 4 ingredients in large bowl. Add pineapple mixture. Stir. Add bread cubes. Stir until coated. Transfer to greased shallow 2 quart casserole. Bake, covered, in 350°F (175°C) oven for 30 minutes. Remove cover. Bake for another 30 minutes until golden and set.

Sprinkle with toasted coconut. Let stand for 10 minutes. Serves 8.

1 serving: *250 Calories; 11 g Total Fat (0 g Mono, 0 g Poly, 9 g Sat); 0 mg Cholesterol; 32 g Carbohydrate; 2 g Fibre; 4 g Protein; 150 mg Sodium*

Couscous Fruit Salad

Did you know that you can beat chilled drained coconut milk solids to a consistency similar to whipped cream? This fruit salad features pretty layers of coconut couscous and fruit, and can be made a day ahead.

Water	1 cup	250 mL
Reserved coconut liquid	2/3 cup	150 mL
Granulated sugar	2 tbsp.	30 mL
Whole-wheat couscous	3/4 cup	175 mL
Can of coconut milk, chilled overnight, drained and liquid reserved	14 oz.	398 mL
Medium sweetened coconut, toasted (see Tip, page 148)	1/2 cup	125 mL
Lime juice	2 tbsp.	30 mL
Chopped frozen mango pieces, thawed	1 1/2 cups	375 mL
Chopped kiwi	1 1/2 cups	375 mL
Sliced fresh strawberries	1 1/2 cups	375 mL

Heat and stir first 3 ingredients in large saucepan on medium-high until boiling. Add couscous. Stir. Remove from heat. Let stand, covered, for 5 minutes. Spread on large plate. Freeze for about 5 minutes until cool.

Spoon chilled coconut solids into large bowl. Beat until stiff peaks form. Fold in toasted coconut, lime juice and couscous. Spread half of mixture in medium (8 cup, 2 L) glass bowl.

Arrange half of remaining 3 ingredients over top. Spread remaining couscous mixture over fruit. Arrange remaining fruit over couscous mixture. Serves 8.

1 serving: *240 Calories; 13 g Total Fat (0.5 g Mono, 0 g Poly, 11 g Sat); 0 mg Cholesterol; 31 g Carbohydrate; 4 g Fibre; 4 g Protein; 20 mg Sodium*

Tofu Noodle Salad

The flavours in this salad are similar to pad thai, with mango adding a lovely sweet element. To make a vegan version, use agave or maple syrup in place of the honey.

Cooking oil	3 tbsp.	45 mL
Rice vinegar	2 tbsp.	30 mL
Liquid honey	1 tbsp.	15 mL
Soy sauce	1 tbsp.	15 mL
Garlic clove, minced	1	1
Finely grated ginger root	1 tsp.	5 mL
Dried crushed chilies	1/8 tsp.	0.5 mL
Package of firm tofu (12.75 oz., 350 g), diced	1/2	1/2
Cooking oil	1 tsp.	5 mL
Rice vermicelli	4 oz.	113 g
Chopped frozen mango pieces, thawed	1 cup	250 mL
Shredded romaine lettuce, lightly packed	1 cup	250 mL
Thinly sliced radish	1/3 cup	75 mL
Chopped fresh cilantro (or parsley)	2 tbsp.	30 mL
Thinly sliced green onion	2 tbsp.	30 mL
Chopped unsalted peanuts	1 tbsp.	15 mL

Whisk first 7 ingredients in medium bowl.

Add tofu. Stir. Chill, covered, for 2 hours, stirring occasionally. Drain, reserving marinade.

Heat medium frying pan on medium-high until very hot. Add second amount of cooking oil. Add tofu. Stir-fry for about 2 minutes until golden. Transfer to large bowl. Let stand for about 20 minutes until cool.

Place vermicelli in large heatproof bowl. Cover with boiling water. Let stand for about 5 minutes until tender. Drain. Rinse with cold water. Drain well. Cut noodles once or twice. Add to tofu.

Add remaining 6 ingredients and reserved marinade. Toss. Makes about 4 1/2 cups (1.1 L).

1 cup (250 mL): *290 Calories; 14 g Total Fat (7 g Mono, 3 g Poly, 1.5 g Sat); 0 mg Cholesterol; 33 g Carbohydrate; 2 g Fibre; 8 g Protein; 210 mg Sodium*

Three-B Salad

Three B's: barley, beans and broccoli! A lively citrus dressing adds vibrant notes to a filling dish fit for any season of the year.

Water	3 cups	750 mL
Salt	3/4 tsp.	4 mL
Pot barley	1 cup	250 mL
Broccoli florets	2 cups	500 mL
Ice water		
Can of mixed beans, rinsed and drained	19 oz.	540 mL
Diced red pepper	1 cup	250 mL
ORANGE CUMIN DRESSING		
Orange juice	1/3 cup	75 mL
Balsamic vinegar	3 tbsp.	45 mL
Grated orange zest (see Tip, page 33)	2 tsp.	10 mL
Brown sugar, packed	1 tsp.	5 mL
Ground cumin	1 tsp.	5 mL
Salt	1/2 tsp.	2 mL
Olive oil	1/3 cup	75 mL

Combine water and salt in large saucepan. Bring to a boil. Add barley. Stir. Reduce heat to medium-low. Cook, covered, for about 1 hour until tender. Drain. Rinse with cold water. Drain well. Transfer to large bowl.

Pour water into large saucepan until about 1 inch (2.5 cm) deep. Add broccoli. Bring to a boil. Reduce heat to medium. Boil gently, covered, for about 3 minutes until tender-crisp. Drain. Plunge broccoli into ice water in medium bowl. Let stand for 10 minutes until cold. Drain. Add to barley.

Add beans and red pepper.

Orange Cumin Dressing: Process first 6 ingredients in blender or food processor until smooth. With motor running, add olive oil in thin stream through hole in lid until slightly thickened. Makes about 3/4 cup (175 mL) dressing. Add to barley mixture. Stir. Makes about 6 cups (1.5 L).

***1 cup (250 mL):** 320 Calories; 13 g Total Fat (9 g Mono, 1.5 g Poly, 2 g Sat); 0 mg Cholesterol; 43 g Carbohydrate; 9 g Fibre; 9 g Protein; 380 mg Sodium*

Garden Shell Salad

An elegant take on a meal salad. These shells, stuffed with a flavourful blend of chickpeas and vegetables, are perfectly suited for a dinner party.

Jumbo shell pasta	20	20
Orange juice	2 tbsp.	30 mL
Red wine vinegar	3 tbsp.	45 mL
Cumin seed, toasted (see Tip, page 148)	2 tsp.	10 mL
Dijon mustard	2 tsp.	10 mL
Granulated sugar	1 tsp.	5 mL
Garlic powder	1/8 tsp.	0.5 mL
Salt, sprinkle		
Olive (or cooking) oil	1/3 cup	75 mL
Olive (or cooking) oil	1 tsp.	5 mL
Chopped onion	1 cup	250 mL
Finely chopped celery	1/2 cup	125 mL
Salt	1/2 tsp.	2 mL
Pepper	1/2 tsp.	2 mL
Chopped fresh spinach leaves, lightly packed	1 1/2 cups	375 mL
Canned chickpeas (garbanzo beans), rinsed and drained, coarsely chopped	1 cup	250 mL
Alfalfa sprouts, lightly packed	1 cup	250 mL
Finely chopped red pepper	1/2 cup	125 mL
Grated orange zest	1/2 tsp.	2 mL

Cook pasta according to package directions. Drain. Rinse with cold water. Drain well.

Process next 7 ingredients in blender or food processor until combined. With motor running, add first amount of olive oil in thin stream through hole in lid until thickened.

Heat second amount of olive oil in large frying pan on medium. Add next 4 ingredients. Cook for about 5 minutes, stirring often, until onion is softened. Add remaining 5 ingredients. Stir. Transfer to large bowl. Let stand until cool. Add orange juice mixture. Toss. Spoon into pasta shells. Makes 20 stuffed shells. Serves 4.

1 serving: *440 Calories; 21 g Total Fat (14 g Mono, 2 g Poly, 3 g Sat); 0 mg Cholesterol; 52 g Carbohydrate; 7 g Fibre; 12 g Protein; 510 mg Sodium*

Asian Cabbage Salad

An attractive, summery salad suitable for a potluck offering. Miso is available in the Asian section of grocery stores or in Asian specialty stores. Look for miso labeled Light, White or Shiro for a mild flavour.

CITRUS MISO DRESSING		
Light miso (fermented soybean paste)	3 tbsp.	45 mL
Lemon juice	2 tbsp.	30 mL
Lime juice	2 tbsp.	30 mL
Cooking oil	1 tbsp.	15 mL
Granulated sugar	1 tbsp.	15 mL
Grated lemon zest (see Tip, below)	1/2 tsp.	2 mL
Grated lime zest	1/2 tsp.	2 mL
Chili paste (sambal oelek)	1/4 tsp.	1 mL
CABBAGE SALAD		
Shredded savoy cabbage, lightly packed	6 cups	1.5 L
Fresh bean sprouts	1 1/2 cups	375 mL
Julienned carrot	1 cup	250 mL
Slivered red pepper	1 cup	250 mL
Sugar snap peas, trimmed and halved	1 cup	250 mL
Sliced green onion	1/4 cup	60 mL
Sesame seeds, toasted	2 tbsp.	30 mL

Citrus Miso Dressing: Process all 8 ingredients in blender until smooth. Makes about 1/2 cup (125 mL) dressing.

Cabbage Salad: Toss first 6 ingredients in large bowl. Add dressing. Toss well.

Sprinkle with sesame seeds. Makes about 10 cups (2.5 L).

1 cup (250 mL): *70 Calories; 3 g Total Fat (1 g Mono, 1 g Poly, 0 g Sat); 0 mg Cholesterol; 10 g Carbohydrate; 3 g Fibre; 3 g Protein; 160 mg Sodium*

tip When a recipe calls for grated lemon zest and juice, it's easier to grate the lemon first, then juice it. Be careful not to grate down to the pith (the white part of the peel), which is bitter and best avoided.

Fennel Coleslaw

The slight licorice flavour of the fennel, sweetness of the dressing and the crunch of the vegetables make this an intriguing coleslaw. If desired, serve with a slotted spoon or tongs to allow most of the marinating dressing to remain in the serving bowl.

Shredded cabbage, lightly packed	**4 cups**	**1 L**
Thinly sliced fennel bulb (white part only), quartered lengthwise first	**3 cups**	**750 mL**
Thinly sliced red pepper	**1 cup**	**250 mL**
Thinly sliced sweet onion	**1 cup**	**250 mL**
Apple cider vinegar	**1/2 cup**	**125 mL**
Granulated sugar	**1/3 cup**	**75 mL**
Fennel seed, crushed	**1/2 tsp.**	**2 mL**
Salt	**1/4 tsp.**	**1 mL**
Pepper	**1/4 tsp.**	**1 mL**

Toss first 4 ingredients in large bowl.

Stir remaining 5 ingredients in small bowl until sugar is dissolved. Pour over cabbage mixture. Stir to coat. Chill, covered, for at least 6 hours or overnight. Makes about 7 cups (1.75 mL).

__1 cup (250 mL):__ 60 Calories; 0 g Total Fat (0 g Mono, 0 g Poly, 0 g Sat); 0 mg Cholesterol; 14 g Carbohydrate; 1 g Fibre; trace Protein; 95 mg Sodium

1. Tomato Shepherd's Pie, page 82
2. Spanakopita Tart, page 76
3. Greek Cannelloni, page 79

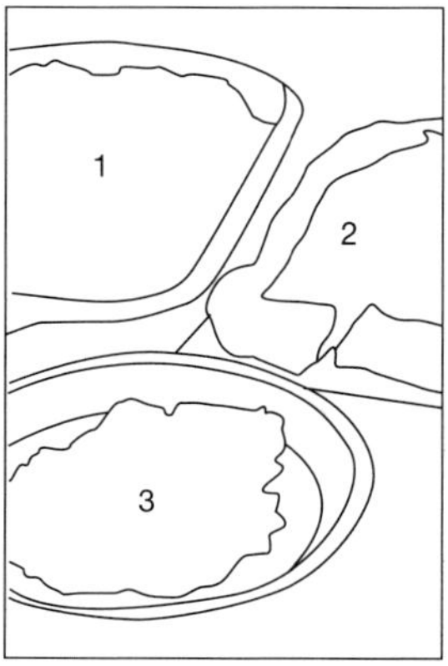

Bean Sprout Salad

Bean sprouts are the main ingredient in this salad with other vegetables in smaller amounts adding crunchy bursts of colour. Try adding any other vegetables that you have on hand.

Fresh bean sprouts	**4 cups**	**1 L**
Frozen French-cut green beans, thawed	**1 cup**	**250 mL**
Thinly sliced red pepper	**1 cup**	**250 mL**
Thinly sliced English cucumber (with peel)	**1 cup**	**250 mL**
Julienned carrot	**1 cup**	**250 mL**
Sliced green onion	**1/4 cup**	**60 mL**
Chopped fresh basil	**2 tbsp.**	**30 mL**
Lime juice	**1/2 cup**	**125 mL**
Fine coconut, toasted	**1/4 cup**	**60 mL**
Brown sugar	**2 tbsp.**	**30 mL**
Chili paste (sambal oelek)	**1 tsp.**	**5 mL**
Salt	**1/2 tsp**	**2 mL**

Combine first 7 ingredients in large bowl.

Process remaining 5 ingredients in blender until smooth. Drizzle over bean sprout mixture. Toss. Makes about 7 cups (1.75 L).

1 cup: *70 Calories; 2.5 g Total Fat (0 g Mono, 0 g Poly, 2 g Sat); 0 mg Cholesterol; 12 g Carbohydrate; 2 g Fibre; 2 g Protein; 200 mg Sodium*

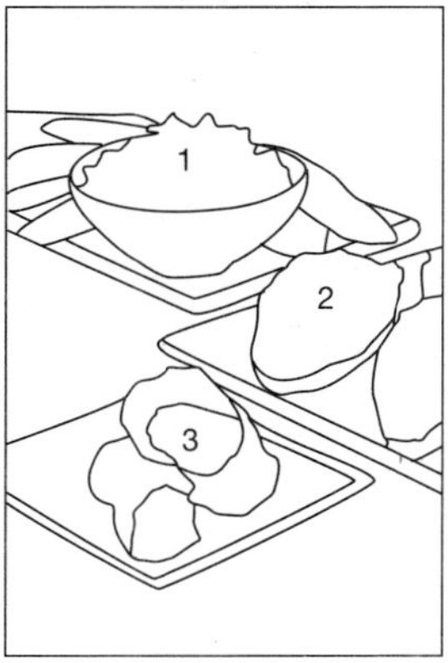

1. Root Vegetable Tapenade, page 16
2. Salsa-stuffed Avocados, page 19
3. Mushroom Salad Rolls, page 14

Avocado Quinoa Salad

VEGAN

A beautiful salad that features protein-rich quinoa, crunchy sunflower seeds, chewy cranberries and creamy avocado. The toasted walnut vinaigrette is a highlight.

Water	1 1/2 cups	375 mL
Salt	1/4 tsp.	1 mL
Quinoa, rinsed and drained	1 cup	250 mL
Diced avocado	1 1/2 cups	375 mL
Chopped spinach leaves, lightly packed	1 cup	250 mL
Finely chopped fennel bulb (white part only)	1 cup	250 mL
Chopped dried cranberries	1/2 cup	125 mL
Unsalted, roasted sunflower seeds	1/4 cup	60 mL
Chopped fresh chives	1 tbsp.	15 mL
WALNUT VINAIGRETTE		
Walnut pieces, toasted (see Tip, page 148)	1/3 cup	75 mL
Olive (or cooking) oil	1/4 cup	60 mL
Lemon juice	2 tbsp.	30 mL
Maple syrup	1 tbsp.	15 mL
Dijon mustard	1 tsp.	5 mL
Salt	1/2 tsp.	2 mL
Pepper	1/4 tsp.	1 mL

Combine water and salt in medium saucepan. Bring to a boil. Add quinoa. Stir. Reduce heat to medium-low. Cook, covered, for about 20 minutes, without stirring, until quinoa is tender. Remove from heat. Let stand, covered, for 5 minutes. Transfer to large bowl. Let stand for about 20 minutes, stirring occasionally, until cool.

Add next 6 ingredients.

Walnut Vinaigrette: Process all 7 ingredients in blender until smooth. Makes about 1/2 cup (125 mL) vinaigrette. Drizzle over quinoa mixture. Stir. Makes about 6 1/2 cups (1.6 L).

1 cup (250 mL): *340 Calories; 21 g Total Fat (10 g Mono, 5 g Poly, 2.5 g Sat); 0 mg Cholesterol; 37 g Carbohydrate; 6 g Fibre; 7 g Protein; 320 mg Sodium*

Pictured on page 71.

Spinach Tabbouleh Salad

Spinach makes a nice addition to the fresh light flavours of tabbouleh. For a gluten-free version, substitute about 1 2/3 cups (400 mL) of cooked quinoa for the bulgur.

Bulgur, fine grind	**1/2 cup**	**125 mL**
Water, to cover		
Finely chopped fresh spinach leaves	**2 cups**	**500 mL**
Diced seeded tomato	**1 cup**	**250 mL**
Finely chopped fresh parsley	**1/2 cup**	**125 mL**
Finely chopped yellow pepper	**1/2 cup**	**125 mL**
Finely chopped fresh mint	**1/4 cup**	**60 mL**
Finely chopped green onion	**1/4 cup**	**60 mL**
Finely chopped radish	**1/4 cup**	**60 mL**
Lemon juice	**1/4 cup**	**60 mL**
Olive oil	**2 tbsp.**	**30 mL**
Salt	**1/2 tsp.**	**2 mL**
Pepper	**1/4 tsp.**	**1 mL**

Cover bulgur with water in small bowl. Stir. Let stand for about 20 minutes until tender. Drain well.

Combine next 7 ingredients in large bowl.

Stir remaining 4 ingredients in small bowl. Drizzle over spinach mixture. Toss. Add bulgur. Stir. Makes about 4 3/4 cups (1.2 L).

3/4 cup (175 mL): *130 Calories; 6 g Total Fat (4 g Mono, 0.5 g Poly, 1 g Sat); 0 mg Cholesterol; 18 g Carbohydrate; 5 g Fibre; 4 g Protein; 280 mg Sodium*

Apple Fig Pita Salad

Crisp golden toasted pitas frame a tossed romaine salad with apple, figs, tomato and almonds. Tahini lends its distinctiveness to the dressing.

LEMON TAHINI DRESSING		
Tahini (sesame paste)	1/4 cup	60 mL
Water	2 tbsp.	30 mL
Lemon juice	1 tbsp.	15 mL
Olive oil	1 tbsp.	15 mL
Grated lemon zest (see Tip, page 33)	1/2 tsp.	2 mL
Salt	1/4 tsp.	1 mL
Pepper	1/4 tsp.	1 mL
PITA SALAD		
Pita breads (7 inch, 18 cm, diameter)	4	4
Olive oil	1 tbsp.	15 mL
Greek seasoning	1 tsp.	5 mL
Romaine lettuce mix	5 cups	1.25 L
Thinly sliced unpeeled tart apple (such as Granny Smith)	1 cup	250 mL
Chopped English cucumber (with peel), 1/2 inch (12 mm) pieces	1/2 cup	125 mL
Halved grape tomatoes	1/2 cup	125 mL
Sliced dried figs	1/2 cup	125 mL
Sliced natural almonds, toasted (see Tip, page 148)	1/4 cup	60 mL

Lemon Tahini Dressing: Whisk all 7 ingredients in small bowl, adding more water if necessary for pourable consistency. Makes about 1/2 cup (125 mL) dressing.

Pita Salad: Brush 1 side of pitas with olive oil. Sprinkle with seasoning. Arrange in single layer on ungreased baking sheet. Bake in 375°F (190°C) oven for about 12 minutes until golden and crisp. Let stand until cool. Break into halves. Arrange on 4 individual plates.

Combine next 5 ingredients in large bowl. Drizzle with Lemon Tahini Dressing. Toss. Arrange over pitas. Sprinkle with almonds. Serves 4.

***1 serving:** 470 Calories; 24 g Total Fat (12 g Mono, 7 g Poly, 3 g Sat); 0 mg Cholesterol; 58 g Carbohydrate; 8 g Fibre; 13 g Protein; 330 mg Sodium*

Pictured on page 71.

Orzo Black Bean Salad

A brightly coloured bean and pasta salad that makes great use of tangy goat cheese, fresh herbs and arugula.

Orzo	**1 cup**	**250 mL**
Lime juice	**1/4 cup**	**60 mL**
Olive (or cooking) oil	**3 tbsp.**	**45 mL**
Liquid honey	**2 tbsp.**	**30 mL**
Dijon mustard	**1 tsp.**	**5 mL**
Dried crushed chilies	**1/2 tsp.**	**2 mL**
Salt	**1/2 tsp.**	**2 mL**
Can of black beans, rinsed and drained	**19 oz.**	**540 mL**
Diced celery	**1 1/2 cups**	**375 mL**
Chopped arugula (or fresh spinach leaves), lightly packed	**1 cup**	**250 mL**
Diced red pepper	**1 cup**	**250 mL**
Goat (chèvre) cheese, cut up	**2 oz.**	**57 g**
Chopped fresh basil	**1 tbsp.**	**15 mL**
Chopped fresh parsley	**1 tbsp.**	**15 mL**
Chopped fresh oregano	**2 tsp.**	**10 mL**

Cook pasta according to package directions. Drain.

Whisk next 6 ingredients in large bowl.

Add remaining 8 ingredients and pasta. Stir. Makes about 7 1/2 cups (1.9 L).

1 cup (250 mL): *250 Calories; 8 g Total Fat (4.5 g Mono, 0.5 g Poly, 2 g Sat); trace Cholesterol; 37 g Carbohydrate; 5 g Fibre; 7 g Protein; 360 mg Sodium*

Pictured on page 71.

Edamame Pepper Soup

Colourful chunks of bell pepper brighten this thick, protein-rich soup.

Prepared vegetable broth	**4 cups**	**1 L**
Chopped onion	**1 cup**	**250 mL**
Frozen shelled edamame (soybeans)	**3 cups**	**750 mL**
Chopped red pepper	**3/4 cup**	**175 mL**
Chopped orange pepper	**3/4 cup**	**175 mL**
Chopped yellow pepper	**3/4 cup**	**175 mL**
Milk	**1 cup**	**250 mL**
Grated jalapeño Monterey Jack cheese	**1 cup**	**250 mL**
Hot pepper sauce	**1/4 tsp.**	**1 mL**

Bring broth and onion to a boil in large saucepan. Add edamame. Reduce heat to medium. Boil gently, uncovered, for 10 minutes. Transfer to blender or food processor. Carefully process until smooth (see Safety Tip). Return to saucepan. Bring to a boil.

Add next 3 ingredients. Stir. Reduce heat to medium-low. Simmer, covered, for about 15 minutes until peppers are tender-crisp.

Add remaining 3 ingredients. Stir until cheese is melted. Makes about 7 1/2 cups (1.9 L).

1 cup (250 mL): *180 Calories; 7 g Total Fat (0 g Mono, 0 g Poly, 2.5 g Sat); 15 mg Cholesterol; 16 g Carbohydrate; 4 g Fibre; 12 g Protein; 470 mg Sodium*

Pictured on page 17.

Safety Tip: Follow manufacturer's instructions for processing hot liquids.

Cabbage Vegetable Soup

This tomato soup, full of soft cabbage and veggies, is nicely seasoned with herbs and spices. It can be stored in an airtight container in the freezer for up to three months.

Cooking oil	1 tsp.	5 mL
Chopped cabbage	3 cups	750 mL
Chopped onion	2 cups	500 mL
Chopped carrot	1 cup	250 mL
Chopped celery	1 cup	250 mL
Prepared vegetable broth	6 cups	1.5 L
Can of diced tomatoes (with juice)	28 oz.	796 mL
Bay leaves	2	2
Dried oregano	1 1/2 tsp.	7 mL
Dried basil	1 tsp.	5 mL
Garlic cloves, minced (or 1/2 tsp., 2 mL, powder)	2	2
Granulated sugar	1/2 tsp.	2 mL
Dried crushed chilies	1/4 tsp.	1 mL
Chopped zucchini (with peel)	1 cup	250 mL
Frozen cut green beans, thawed	1 cup	250 mL

Heat cooking oil in Dutch oven on medium. Add next 4 ingredients. Cook for about 15 minutes, stirring occasionally, until cabbage is softened.

Add next 8 ingredients. Stir. Simmer, covered, for about 1 hour until vegetables are tender.

Add zucchini and green beans. Stir. Cook, covered, for about 10 minutes until zucchini is tender-crisp. Remove and discard bay leaves. Makes about 13 cups (3.25 L).

1 cup (250 mL): *45 Calories; 0 g Total Fat (0 g Mono, 0 g Poly, 0 g Sat); 0 mg Cholesterol; 10 g Carbohydrate; 2 g Fibre; 2 g Protein; 480 mg Sodium*

Beat the Clock Borscht

Making borscht is usually an involved and lengthy process but this version is ready in 30 minutes! Delicious hot or cold.

Cooking oil	**1 tsp.**	**5 mL**
Coleslaw mix	**2 cups**	**500 mL**
Chopped onion	**1 cup**	**250 mL**
Prepared vegetable broth	**4 cups**	**1 L**
Pepper	**1/4 tsp.**	**1 mL**
Cans of sliced beets (14 oz., 398 mL, each), with juice	**2**	**2**
Can of baked beans in tomato sauce	**14 oz.**	**398 mL**
Sour cream	**1/4 cup**	**60 mL**
Chopped fresh dill	**1 tbsp.**	**15 mL**
Lemon juice	**2 tsp.**	**10 mL**

Heat cooking oil in Dutch oven on medium-high. Add coleslaw mix and onion. Cook, covered, for about 3 minutes, stirring occasionally, until onion is softened and browned.

Add broth and pepper. Process beets with juice and baked beans in blender or food processor until smooth. Add to broth mixture. Stir. Bring to a boil. Reduce heat to medium-low. Simmer, covered, for 10 minutes. Remove from heat.

Stir in remaining 3 ingredients. Makes about 9 1/4 cups (2.3 L).

1 cup (250 mL): *110 Calories; 2 g Total Fat (0.5 g Mono, 0 g Poly, 1 g Sat); trace Cholesterol; 20 g Carbohydrate; 4 g Fibre; 4 g Protein; 600 mg Sodium*

Maestro's Minestrone

Wave your wooden spoon baton through this symphony of simple vegetables and hearty grains. Garnish with Parmesan cheese and fresh basil.

Olive (or cooking) oil	1 tbsp.	15 mL
Chopped carrot	1 cup	250 mL
Chopped celery	1 cup	250 mL
Chopped fennel bulb (white part only)	1 cup	250 mL
Chopped onion	1 cup	250 mL
Dried crushed chilies (optional)	1/8 tsp.	0.5 mL
Water	8 cups	2 L
Can of diced tomatoes (with juice)	28 oz.	796 mL
Can of chickpeas (garbanzo beans), rinsed and drained	19 oz.	540 mL
Can of romano beans, rinsed and drained	19 oz.	540 mL
Can of tomato paste	5 1/2 oz.	156 mL
Pot barley	1/2 cup	125 mL
Dried oregano	1 tsp.	5 mL
Bay leaf	1	1
Chopped kale leaves, lightly packed	3 cups	750 mL
Salt	1/2 tsp.	2 mL
Basil pesto	1/4 cup	60 mL
Balsamic vinegar	2 tbsp.	30 mL

Heat olive oil in a Dutch oven on medium. Add next 5 ingredients. Cook for about 10 minutes, stirring occasionally, until vegetables are golden.

Add next 8 ingredients. Stir. Bring to a boil. Reduce heat to medium-low. Simmer, covered, for about 40 minutes, stirring occasionally, until barley is tender.

Add kale and salt. Stir. Simmer, covered, for about 10 minutes until kale is tender.

Stir in pesto and vinegar. Makes about 15 cups (3.75 L).

1 cup (250 mL): *140 Calories; 3.5 g Total Fat (0.5 g Mono, 0 g Poly, 0.5 g Sat); 0 mg Cholesterol; 23 g Carbohydrate; 5 g Fibre; 6 g Protein; 400 mg Sodium*

Pumpkin Coconut Soup

Using pumpkin purée and coconut milk eliminates the need for flour for thickening, which makes this oh-so-simple soup gluten-free. Top with a sprinkle of chopped roasted cashews and cilantro.

Vegetable cocktail juice	2 cups	500 mL
Can of coconut milk	14 oz.	398 mL
Can of pure pumpkin (no spices)	14 oz.	398 mL
Chili paste (sambal oelek)	1 tsp.	5 mL
Garlic clove, minced (or 1/2 tsp., 2 mL, powder)	1	1

Whisk all 5 ingredients in large saucepan until smooth. Bring to a boil, stirring occasionally. Reduce heat to medium-low. Simmer, uncovered, for 10 minutes, stirring occasionally, to blend flavours. Makes about 4 3/4 cups (1.2 L).

1 cup (250 mL): *200 Calories; 18 g Total Fat (1 g Mono, 0 g Poly, 16 g Sat); 0 mg Cholesterol; 10 g Carbohydrate; 3 g Fibre; 3 g Protein; 280 mg Sodium*

Vegetable Wonton Soup

Lentils replace the meat usually found in the filling of wontons.

Chinese dried mushrooms	6	6
Canned lentils, rinsed and drained, coarsely mashed	1 cup	250 mL
Finely chopped bok choy	1 cup	250 mL
Chopped canned water chestnuts	1/4 cup	60 mL
Cornstarch	2 tbsp.	30 mL
Soy sauce	2 tbsp.	30 mL
Finely grated ginger root (or 3/4 tsp., 4 mL, ground ginger)	2 tsp.	10 mL
Rice vinegar	2 tsp.	10 mL
Sesame oil	1 tsp.	5 mL
Pepper	1/4 tsp.	1 mL

(continued on next page)

Wonton wrappers	**32**	**32**
Prepared vegetable broth	**6 cups**	**1.5 L**
Water	**2 cups**	**500 mL**
Ginger root slices (1/8 inch, 3 mm, thick)	**3**	**3**
Star anise	**2**	**2**
Chopped green onion	**1/4 cup**	**60 mL**

Put mushrooms into small heatproof bowl. Add boiling water. Stir. Let stand for about 20 minutes until softened. Drain. Squeeze to remove excess liquid. Remove and discard stems. Finely chop mushrooms. Transfer to large bowl.

Add next 9 ingredients. Stir well.

Lay 1 wrapper on work surface with 1 corner closest to you. Keep unused wrappers covered with damp tea towel to prevent drying. Place about 2 tsp. (10 mL) filling in middle of wrapper. Brush edges of wrapper with water. Fold up 1 corner to meet opposite corner, forming triangle. Gather edges together to form pleats and press firmly to seal. Repeat with remaining filling and wrappers, keeping filled wontons covered with damp tea towel. Makes 32 wontons.

Combine next 4 ingredients in large saucepan. Bring to a boil. Reduce heat to medium. Remove ginger and star anise. Add wontons. Simmer, uncovered, for 10 minutes, stirring occasionally. Add green onion. Makes about 9 1/2 cups (2.4 L). Serves 4.

1 serving: *130 Calories; 1 g Total Fat (0 g Mono, 0 g Poly, 0 g Sat); trace Cholesterol; 25 g Carbohydrate; 2 g Fibre; 5 g Protein; 760 mg Sodium*

Chipotle Corn Chowder

A full-bodied corn chowder without dairy or flour. The smoky chipotle *heat is well balanced by sweet corn and potatoes.*

Cooking oil	**2 tsp.**	**10 mL**
Chopped peeled potato	**2 cups**	**500 mL**
Chopped celery	**1 cup**	**250 mL**
Chopped onion	**1 cup**	**250 mL**
Finely chopped chipotle peppers in adobo sauce (see Tip, page 61)	**2 tsp.**	**10 mL**
Garlic cloves, minced (or 1/2 tsp., 2 mL, powder)	**2**	**2**
Dried oregano	**1/2 tsp.**	**2 mL**
Salt	**1/4 tsp.**	**1 mL**
Pepper	**1/4 tsp.**	**1 mL**
Prepared vegetable broth	**6 cups**	**1.5 L**
Fresh (or frozen, thawed) kernel corn	**4 cups**	**1 L**
Chopped fresh cilantro (or parsley)	**2 tbsp.**	**30 mL**

Heat cooking oil in a Dutch oven on medium-high. Add next 3 ingredients. Cook for about 5 minutes, stirring occasionally, until celery is softened.

Add next 5 ingredients. Heat and stir for about 1 minute until garlic is fragrant.

Add broth and corn. Bring to a boil. Reduce heat to medium-low. Boil gently, covered, for 15 minutes until potato is tender. Remove half of mixture to blender or food processor. Carefully process until smooth (see Safety Tip). Return to remaining corn mixture.

Stir in cilantro. Makes about 10 cups (2.5 L).

1 cup (250 mL): *80 Calories; 2 g Total Fat (0.5 g Mono, 0 g Poly, 0 g Sat); 0 mg Cholesterol; 17 g Carbohydrate; 2 g Fibre; 2 g Protein; 420 mg Sodium*

Pictured on page 107.

Safety Tip: Follow manufacturer's instructions for processing hot liquids.

Swiss Chard Soup

Plenty of vegetables and beans in a tasty broth make this a filling meal. Serve with crusty whole-grain rolls.

Olive (or cooking) oil	**1 tbsp.**	**15 mL**
Chopped fennel bulb (white part only)	**1 cup**	**250 mL**
Chopped leek (white part only)	**1 cup**	**250 mL**
Diced carrot	**1 cup**	**250 mL**
Garlic cloves, minced (or 3/4 tsp., 4 mL, powder)	**3**	**3**
Prepared vegetable broth	**8 cups**	**2 L**
Can of navy beans, rinsed and drained	**19 oz.**	**540 mL**
Dried thyme	**1/2 tsp.**	**2 mL**
Dried crushed chilies	**1/2 tsp.**	**2 mL**
Chopped Swiss chard (leaves and stems), lightly packed	**4 cups**	**1 L**
Chopped fresh parsley	**2 tbsp.**	**30 mL**
Lemon juice	**1 tbsp.**	**15 mL**

Heat olive oil in a Dutch oven on medium. Add next 4 ingredients. Cook for about 10 minutes, stirring occasionally, until fennel is softened.

Add next 4 ingredients. Stir. Bring to a boil. Reduce heat to medium-low. Simmer, covered, for 15 minutes.

Add Swiss chard. Stir. Cook, covered, for about 12 minutes until tender.

Stir in parsley and lemon juice. Makes about 11 cups (2.75 L).

1 cup (250 mL): *50 Calories; 1.5 g Total Fat (1 g Mono, 0 g Poly, 0 g Sat); 0 mg Cholesterol; 8 g Carbohydrate; 3 g Fibre; 2 g Protein; 110 mg Sodium*

Pictured on page 17.

Tomato Lentil Soup

A hearty, savoury soup, with just a hint of curry and tomato sweetness—it will warm you to the core on a chilly afternoon. Add a sprinkle of freshly ground pepper if desired.

Prepared vegetable broth	**6 cups**	**1.5 L**
Dried red split lentils	**2 cups**	**500 mL**
Can of stewed tomatoes, cut up	**14 oz.**	**398 mL**
Curry powder	**1 tsp.**	**5 mL**
Lemon juice	**1 tsp.**	**5 mL**

Combine first 4 ingredients in large saucepan. Bring to a boil. Reduce heat to medium-low. Simmer, covered, for about 25 minutes, stirring occasionally, until lentils are tender.

Stir in lemon juice. Makes about 8 cups (2 L).

__1 cup (250 mL):__ 190 Calories; 1 g Total Fat (0 g Mono, 0 g Poly, 0 g Sat); 0 mg Cholesterol; 33 g Carbohydrate; 7 g Fibre; 13 g Protein; 590 mg Sodium

Pictured on page 17.

Thai Hot and Sour Soup

A pleasing light soup with plenty of vegetables and a nice chili heat. Cut veggies on an angle for a pretty look. You can substitute fresh shiitake and oyster mushrooms for the brown mushrooms for a slightly different taste.

Cooking oil	**2 tsp.**	**10 mL**
Sliced fresh brown (or white) mushrooms	**4 cups**	**1 L**
Garlic clove, minced (or 1/4 tsp., 1 mL, powder)	**1**	**1**
Prepared vegetable broth	**6 cups**	**1.5 L**
Thinly sliced carrot	**1 cup**	**250 mL**
Thinly sliced celery	**1 cup**	**250 mL**
Finely chopped fresh hot chili pepper (see Tip, page 51)	**1 tsp.**	**5 mL**
Finely grated ginger root (or 3/4 tsp., 4 mL, ground ginger)	**1 tbsp.**	**15 mL**

(continued on next page)

Lemon grass paste (or 1 tbsp., 15 mL, finely chopped lemon grass bulb)	1 tbsp.	15 mL
Snow peas, trimmed and halved	1 cup	250 mL
Package of firm tofu (12.75 oz., 350 g), cut into 1/2 inch (12 mm) pieces	1/2	1/2
Lime juice	3 tbsp.	45 mL
Cornstarch	2 tbsp.	30 mL
Soy sauce	2 tbsp.	30 mL
Granulated sugar	1 tbsp.	15 mL
Sliced green onion	1/4 cup	60 mL
Chopped fresh basil	2 tbsp.	30 mL

Heat cooking oil in large saucepan or Dutch oven on medium. Add mushrooms and garlic. Cook for about 10 minutes, stirring occasionally, until mushrooms are browned. Add next 6 ingredients. Bring to a boil. Reduce heat to medium-low. Simmer, covered, for about 5 minutes, stirring occasionally, until vegetables are tender-crisp.

Add snow peas and tofu. Bring to a boil.

Stir next 4 ingredients in small bowl until smooth. Add to vegetable mixture. Heat and stir for about 1 minute until boiling and thickened.

Sprinkle green onion and basil on individual servings. Makes about 9 1/4 cups (2.3 L).

1 cup (250 mL): *80 Calories; 3 g Total Fat (0.5 g Mono, 0 g Poly, 0 g Sat); 0 mg Cholesterol; 10 g Carbohydrate; trace Fibre; 4 g Protein; 630 mg Sodium*

Pictured on page 72.

tip Hot peppers contain capsaicin in the seeds and ribs. Removing the seeds and ribs will reduce the heat. Wear rubber gloves when handling hot peppers and avoid touching your eyes. Wash your hands well afterwards.

Almond Apple Chèvre Toasts

A unique combination of flavours that will surprise and delight.

Almond butter	**1/4 cup**	**60 mL**
Dried cranberries, chopped	**2 tbsp.**	**30 mL**
Whole-wheat bread slices, toasted	**8**	**8**
Thinly sliced red onion	**2 tbsp.**	**30 mL**
Thinly sliced peeled tart apple (such as Granny Smith)	**1 cup**	**250 mL**
Goat (chèvre) cheese	**4 oz.**	**113 g**
Liquid honey	**1 tbsp.**	**15 mL**

Combine almond butter and cranberries in small bowl. Spread on 4 toast slices. Scatter onion over top. Arrange apple over onion.

Stir goat cheese and honey in separate small bowl until combined. Spread on remaining 4 bread slices. Place over apple, goat cheese–side down. Cut in half diagonally. Makes 4 sandwiches.

1 sandwich: *480 Calories; 20 g Total Fat (2.5 g Mono, 3 g Poly, 5 g Sat); 15 mg Cholesterol; 63 g Carbohydrate; 8 g Fibre; 17 g Protein; 420 mg Sodium*

1. Veggie Rainbow Wraps, page 58
2. Western Portobello Burgers, page 56
3. Cheesy Chickpea Melt, page 62

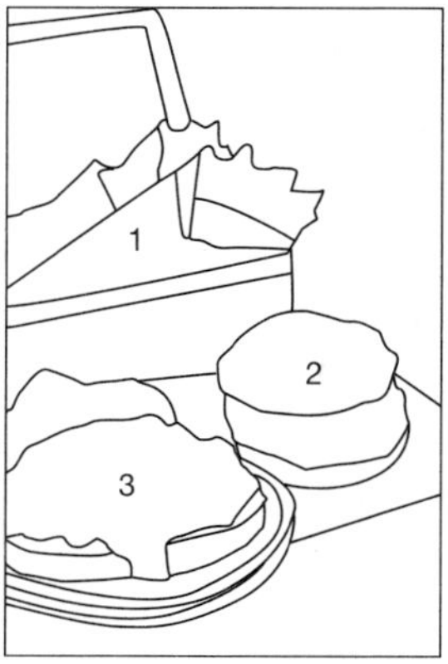

CLUB

Avocado Onion Bunwiches

The slight nip of blue cheese and tang of lemon make this bunwich interesting. Consider adding other vegetables, such as sliced cucumbers or alfalfa sprouts, for additional crunch and flavour.

Block cream cheese, softened	**4 oz.**	**125 g**
Crumbled blue cheese	**1/4 cup**	**60 mL**
Sliced green onion	**2 tbsp.**	**30 mL**
Lemon juice	**1 tsp.**	**5 mL**
Pepper	**1/4 tsp.**	**1 mL**
Onion buns, split	**4**	**4**
Spring mix lettuce, lightly packed	**1 cup**	**250 mL**
Thinly sliced unpeeled tart apple (such as Granny Smith)	**1/2 cup**	**125 mL**
Large avocadoes, sliced	**2**	**2**

Combine first 5 ingredients in small bowl.

Spread cheese mixture on bun halves. Layer next 3 ingredients, in order given, on bottom half of each bun. Cover with top halves. Makes 4 bunwiches.

1 bunwich: *420 Calories; 27 g Total Fat (9 g Mono, 1.5 g Poly, 10 g Sat); 35 mg Cholesterol; 39 g Carbohydrate; 7 g Fibre; 11 g Protein; 430 mg Sodium*

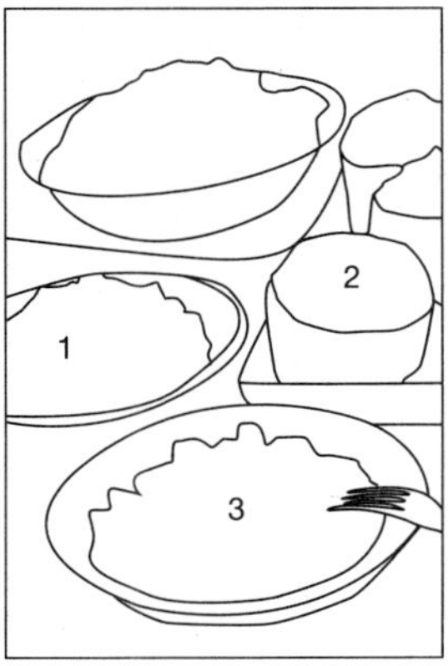

1. Caribbean Vegetable Rice, page 105
2. Spanish Stuffed Peppers, page 99
3. Veggie Meatball Stew, page 109

Western Portobello Burgers

A portobello mushroom filled with scrambled eggs, smothered in melted cheese, topped with crispy lettuce on a toasted kaiser roll... what more could you want?

Portobello mushrooms, stems and gills removed (see Tip, page 72)	**4**	**4**
Cooking oil	**1 tsp.**	**5 mL**
Diced green pepper	**1/2 cup**	**125 mL**
Diced onion	**1/2 cup**	**125 mL**
Large eggs	**4**	**4**
Milk	**1/4 cup**	**60 mL**
Salt	**1/4 tsp.**	**1 mL**
Pepper	**1/4 tsp.**	**1 mL**
Deli sharp Cheddar cheese slices	**4**	**4**
Lettuce leaves	**4**	**4**
Whole-wheat kaiser rolls, split and toasted	**4**	**4**

Arrange mushrooms, stem-side up, on microwave-safe plate. Microwave on high (100%) for about 3 minutes until softened (see Tip, page 133). Place stem-side up in greased 9 x 13 inch (23 x 33 cm) pan.

Heat cooking oil in large frying pan on medium. Add green pepper and onion. Cook for about 8 minutes, stirring often, until pepper is softened.

Whisk next 4 ingredients in medium bowl. Pour over onion mixture. Reduce heat to medium-low. Stir slowly with spatula while egg is starting to set, scraping sides and bottom of pan until almost cooked but still wet. Spoon egg mixture into mushrooms.

Arrange cheese slices over egg mixture. Cover with greased foil. Bake in 350°F (175°C) oven for about 20 minutes until mushrooms are tender and cheese is melted.

Serve mushrooms, topped with lettuce, in rolls. Makes 4 mushroom burgers.

***1 mushroom burger:** 350 Calories; 13 g Total Fat (2.5 g Mono, 1 g Poly, 6 g Sat); 160 mg Cholesterol; 39 g Carbohydrate; 6 g Fibre; 20 g Protein; 750 mg Sodium*

Pictured on page 53.

"BLT" Baguette Bake

A modern vegetarian take on the traditional BLT—Beans, Leeks and Tomato with tangy blue cheese. These open-faced sandwiches make a lovely casual brunch dish.

Cooking oil	**1 tsp.**	**5 mL**
Thinly sliced leek (white part only)	**2 cups**	**500 mL**
All-purpose flour	**2 tbsp.**	**30 mL**
Salt	**1/4 tsp.**	**1 mL**
Coarsely ground pepper	**1/2 tsp.**	**2 mL**
Prepared vegetable broth	**3/4 cup**	**175 mL**
Can of romano beans, rinsed and drained	**19 oz.**	**540 mL**
Whole-wheat baguette bread loaf, split	**1**	**1**
Crumbled blue cheese	**1/3 cup**	**75 mL**
Diced seeded tomato	**1 cup**	**250 mL**

Heat cooking oil in large frying pan on medium. Add leeks. Cook for about 8 minutes, stirring often, until softened.

Add next 3 ingredients. Heat and stir for 1 minute. Slowly add broth, stirring constantly until smooth. Heat and stir until boiling and thickened.

Coarsely mash half of the beans. Add to pan with remaining beans. Cook for about 5 minutes, stirring occasionally, until heated through. Remove from heat.

Cut each bread loaf half into 3 pieces. Arrange, cut-side up, in ungreased 9 x 13 inch (23 x 33 cm) baking pan, trimming to fit if necessary. Spoon bean mixture over top.

Scatter cheese over bean mixture. Bake in 375°F (190°C) oven for about 20 minutes until cheese is melted and edges of bread are golden.

Scatter tomato over top. Makes 6 open-faced sandwiches.

***1 open-faced sandwich:** 220 Calories; 4 g Total Fat (1 g Mono, 0 g Poly, 2 g Sat); 5 mg Cholesterol; 34 g Carbohydrate; 7 g Fibre; 11 g Protein; 690 mg Sodium*

Variation: Use a milder cheese like Swiss or havarti in place of blue cheese.

Veggie Rainbow Wraps

A beautiful array of veggies and a creamy spread make these vegan wraps really stand out.

Grated carrot	3/4 cup	175 mL
Tahini (sesame paste)	1/2 cup	125 mL
Finely grated ginger root (or 1/4 tsp., 1 mL, ground ginger)	1 tsp.	5 mL
Salt	1/8 tsp.	0.5 mL
Pepper	1/4 tsp.	1 mL
Spinach tortillas (9 inch, 23 cm, diameter)	4	4
Romaine lettuce leaves	4	4
Thinly sliced yellow pepper	1 cup	250 mL
Sliced tomato	1 cup	250 mL
Sliced English cucumber (with peel)	1 cup	250 mL

Combine first 5 ingredients in small bowl.

Spread carrot mixture on tortillas. Layer remaining ingredients, in order given, over carrot mixture. Fold bottom over filling. Fold sides over. Secure with wooden picks. Makes 4 wraps.

1 wrap: *430 Calories; 21 g Total Fat (8 g Mono, 8 g Poly, 3.5 g Sat); 0 mg Cholesterol; 52 g Carbohydrate; 7 g Fibre; 12 g Protein; 470 mg Sodium*

Pictured on page 53.

Fresh Falafel Wraps

Authentic falafel taste but lighter than the normal deep-fried version. This recipe makes enough falafel for 6 wraps. Patties can cooked and frozen. Gently reheat in the oven or microwave and proceed with filling pitas.

FALAFEL

Can of chickpeas (garbanzo beans), rinsed and drained	19 oz.	540 mL
Cooked long-grain brown rice (about 1/3 cup, 75 mL, uncooked)	1 cup	250 mL
Tahini (sesame paste)	1/2 cup	125 mL

(continued on next page)

Garlic cloves, minced (or 1/2 tsp., 2 mL, powder)	2	2
Dried mint leaves	1 tbsp.	15 mL
Salt	3/4 tsp.	4 mL
Pepper	1/4 tsp.	1 mL
Olive (or cooking) oil	2 tbsp.	30 mL

TAHINI SAUCE

Tahini (sesame paste)	1/4 cup	60 mL
Lemon juice	2 tbsp.	30 mL
Ground allspice	1/8 tsp.	0.5 mL
Water	2 tbsp.	30 mL

WRAPS

Pita breads (7 inch, 18 cm, diameter)	6	6
Romaine lettuce leaves	6	6
Large tomato slices, halved	6	6
Thinly sliced red onion	1/4 cup	60 mL

Falafel: Process first 7 ingredients in food processor with on/off motion until combined but not too smooth. Form into balls, using about 2 tbsp. (30 mL) for each. Flatten to 1/2 inch (12 mm) thickness. Heat 1 tbsp. (15 mL) olive oil in large frying pan on medium. Add half of patties. Cook for about 4 minutes per side until golden brown and heated through. Wipe pan with paper towel. Repeat with remaining cooking oil and patties. Makes about 18 falafel.

Tahini Sauce: Stir all 4 ingredients in small bowl until smooth. Makes about 1/2 cup (125 mL).

Wraps: Place pitas on ungreased baking sheet. Bake in 350°F (175°C) oven for about 2 minutes until softened. Spread Tahini Sauce on pitas. Arrange lettuce in centre of pitas. Top with falafels, tomato and onion. Fold bottom over filling. Fold sides over. Serve immediately. Makes 6 wraps.

__1 wrap:__ 550 Calories; 22 g Total Fat (9 g Mono, 7 g Poly, 3 g Sat); 0 mg Cholesterol; 72 g Carbohydrate; 11 g Fibre; 18 g Protein; 620 mg Sodium

Smoky Black Bean Burgers

Vibrant southwestern flavours in a satisfying vegan burger. Shape the patties on a piece of waxed paper to make it easier to lift and transfer them to the frying pan.

Cooking oil	1 tsp.	5 mL
Chopped onion	1 cup	250 mL
Garlic cloves, minced (or 3/4 tsp., 4 mL, powder)	3	3
Finely chopped chipotle peppers in adobo sauce (see Tip, page 61)	1 tsp.	5 mL
Chili powder	1 tbsp.	15 mL
Salt	1/4 tsp.	1 mL
Can of black beans, rinsed and drained	19 oz.	540 mL
Cooked long-grain brown rice (or 3/4 cup, 175 mL, uncooked)	2 1/2 cups	625 mL
Cooking oil	1 tbsp.	15 mL
Large avocado	1	1
Salsa	2 tbsp.	30 mL
Lime juice	2 tsp.	10 mL
Multi-grain (or whole-wheat) hamburger buns, split	6	6
Large tomato slices	6	6
Small yellow pepper, cut crosswise into rings	1	1

Heat first amount of cooking oil in large frying pan on medium. Add next 5 ingredients. Cook for about 5 minutes, stirring occasionally, until onion is softened. Transfer to large bowl.

Coarsely mash half of beans in small bowl. Add to onion. Add rice and remaining beans. Mix well. Divide into 6 equal portions. Shape into 1/2 inch (12 mm) thick patties.

Heat second amount of cooking oil in same frying pan on medium. Cook patties for about 3 minutes per side until golden brown and heated through.

(continued on next page)

Mash next 3 ingredients in small bowl. Spread avocado mixture onto bun halves.

Serve patties, topped with tomato and yellow pepper, in buns. Makes 6 burgers.

__1 burger:__ 430 Calories; 10 g Total Fat (4.5 g Mono, 1.5 g Poly, 1.5 g Sat); 0 mg Cholesterol; 73 g Carbohydrate; 12 g Fibre; 17 g Protein; 740 mg Sodium

Pictured on page 126.

tip Chipotle chili peppers are smoked jalapeno peppers. Be sure to wash your hands after handling. To store any leftover chipotle chili peppers, divide into recipe-friendly portions and freeze, with sauce, in airtight containers for up to one year.

VEGAN

Chili Tofu Wraps

Warm slices of tofu are seasoned and glazed with sweet chili sauce in these leafy wraps.

Package of firm tofu, quartered lengthwise	**12.75 oz.**	**350 g**
Sweet chili sauce	**1/2 cup**	**125 mL**
Shredded romaine lettuce leaves, lightly packed	**2 cups**	**500 mL**
Sliced red pepper	**1 cup**	**250 mL**
Whole-wheat flour tortillas	**4**	**4**

Pour chili sauce over tofu in pie plate. Let stand, covered, in refrigerator for 30 minutes, turning once. Using slotted spoon, transfer tofu to greased baking sheet with sides. Reserve remaining sauce. Bake in 450°F (230°C) oven for about 20 minutes, turning at halftime, until golden brown. Transfer to remaining sauce. Turn to coat.

Arrange lettuce and red pepper along centre of tortillas, leaving 1 inch (2.5 cm) edge at bottom. Place tofu over top. Fold bottom over filling. Fold sides over. Makes 4 wraps.

__1 wrap:__ 370 Calories; 11 g Total Fat (0 g Mono, 0 g Poly, 2.5 g Sat); 0 mg Cholesterol; 49 g Carbohydrate; 5 g Fibre; 18 g Protein; 710 mg Sodium

Pictured on page 144.

Cheesy Chickpea Melt

A great substitute for a tuna melt that makes a quick and easy lunch. Serve with chips.

Can of chickpeas (garbanzo beans), rinsed and drained	**19 oz.**	**540 mL**
Diced celery	**1/2 cup**	**125 mL**
Diced red pepper	**1/4 cup**	**60 mL**
Mayonnaise	**1/4 cup**	**60 mL**
Chopped green onion	**2 tbsp.**	**30 mL**
Salt	**1/4 tsp.**	**1 mL**
Pepper	**1/4 tsp.**	**1 mL**
Rye bread slices, toasted	**4**	**4**
Deli sharp Cheddar cheese slices	**4**	**4**

Coarsely mash chickpeas in medium bowl.

Add next 6 ingredients. Stir.

Arrange rye toast on greased baking sheet. Spread chickpea mixture on toast. Cover with cheese. Broil on centre rack for about 5 minutes until cheese is melted and starting to brown. Makes 4 melts.

1 melt: *330 Calories; 16 g Total Fat (7 g Mono, 3.5 g Poly, 4 g Sat); 20 mg Cholesterol; 33 g Carbohydrate; 6 g Fibre; 11 g Protein; 800 mg Sodium*

Pictured on page 53.

VEGAN

Pepper Aioli Baguette

Sweet, tangy roasted peppers and garlicky white bean aioli combine beautifully with peppery arugula and a whole-wheat baguette.

Large red pepper, cut in 1/4 inch (6 mm) strips	1	1
Large orange pepper, cut in 1/4 inch (6 mm) strips	1	1
Olive oil	1 tbsp.	15 mL
Balsamic vinegar	1 tbsp.	15 mL
Can of navy beans, rinsed and drained	19 oz.	540 mL
Chopped pecans, toasted (see Tip, page 148)	1/2 cup	125 mL
Prepared vegetable broth (or water)	1/4 cup	60 mL
Lemon juice	1 tbsp.	15 mL
Garlic cloves, chopped	2	2
Dried crushed chilies	1/2 tsp.	2 mL
Salt	1/4 tsp.	1 mL
Whole-wheat baguette, split	1	1
Arugula (or spinach leaves), lightly packed	1 1/2 cups	375 mL

Toss first 4 ingredients in large bowl. Arrange in single layer on greased baking sheet. Bake in 425°F (220°C) oven for about 20 minutes until tender and browned. Let stand until cool.

Process next 7 ingredients in food processor until smooth.

Spread bean mixture on baguette halves. Scatter arugula over bottom half of baguette. Arrange roasted peppers over arugula. Cover with top half of baguette. Cut into 4 pieces.

__1 piece:__ 400 Calories; 17 g Total Fat (9 g Mono, 4 g Poly, 2 g Sat); 0 mg Cholesterol; 52 g Carbohydrate; 11 g Fibre; 13 g Protein; 660 mg Sodium

Pictured on page 144.

Couscous Chickpea Burgers

Quick-to-make burgers with hummus flavours and a potato cake texture.

Prepared vegetable broth	**1 cup**	**250 mL**
Couscous	**1/2 cup**	**125 mL**
Dried oregano	**1 tsp.**	**5 mL**
Large egg	**1**	**1**
Can of chickpeas (garbanzo beans), rinsed and drained	**19 oz.**	**540 mL**
Seasoned croutons	**1 cup**	**250 mL**
Chopped green onion	**1/4 cup**	**60 mL**
Garlic clove, minced (or 1/4 tsp., 1 mL, powder)	**1**	**1**
Lemon juice	**1 tbsp.**	**15 mL**
Grated lemon zest	**1 tsp.**	**5 mL**
Ground cumin	**1/2 tsp.**	**2 mL**
Salt	**1/4 tsp**	**1 mL**
Pepper	**1/4 tsp.**	**1 mL**
Cooking oil	**2 tsp.**	**10 mL**
Ranch dressing	**1/4 cup**	**60 mL**
Hamburger buns	**4**	**4**
Tomato slices	**8**	**8**
Dill pickle slices	**8**	**8**

Bring broth to a boil in small saucepan. Add couscous and oregano. Stir. Remove from heat. Let stand, covered, for 5 minutes. Transfer to large bowl.

Process next 10 ingredients in blender or food processor until chickpeas are coarsely chopped. Add to couscous mixture. Mix well. Using about 3/4 cup (175 mL) for each, shape into four 1/2 inch (12 mm) thick patties.

Heat cooking oil in large frying pan on medium. Cook patties for about 4 minutes per side until golden.

Spread dressing on buns. Serve patties, topped with tomato and pickles, in buns. Makes 4 burgers.

***1 burger:** 570 Calories; 18 g Total Fat (3.5 g Mono, 2 g Poly, 3 g Sat); 40 mg Cholesterol; 84 g Carbohydrate; 12 g Fibre; 21 g Protein; 1460 mg Sodium*

Grilled Empanadas

Bread pockets with a tangy, cheesy potato filling. An easy-to-make lunch or after-school snack.

Olive (or cooking) oil	**1 tbsp.**	**15 mL**
Diced potato	**2 cups**	**500 mL**
Chopped onion	**1 1/2 cups**	**375 mL**
Chopped green olives	**1/2 cup**	**125 mL**
Chopped raisins	**1/2 cup**	**125 mL**
Ketchup	**3 tbsp.**	**45 mL**
Red wine vinegar	**1 tbsp.**	**15 mL**
Garlic cloves, minced	**2**	**2**
Paprika	**1 tsp.**	**5 mL**
Ground cumin	**1 tsp.**	**5 mL**
Dried oregano	**1/2 tsp.**	**2 mL**
Salt	**1/2 tsp.**	**2 mL**
Pepper	**1/4 tsp.**	**1 mL**
Grated Mexican cheese blend	**1 cup**	**250 mL**
Frozen dinner roll dough, covered, thawed in refrigerator overnight	**12**	**12**

Heat olive oil in large frying pan on medium. Add potato and onion. Cook for 10 to 15 minutes, stirring often, until potato is tender. Add next 10 ingredients. Cook for about 5 minutes, stirring occasionally, until heated through. Remove from heat. Let stand for about 10 minutes.

Add cheese. Stir.

Roll out each dough portion on lightly floured surface to 6 inch (15 cm) circle. Spoon about 1/4 cup (60 mL) potato mixture in centre of each circle, leaving 1/2 inch (12 mm) edge. Brush edges with water. Fold dough over filling. Pinch edges to seal. Arrange on greased foil-lined baking sheet. Cover with greased waxed paper and tea towel. Let stand in oven with light on and door closed for about 30 minutes until doubled in bulk. To preheat barbecue, turn on one burner. Adjust burner to maintain interior barbecue temperature of medium. Transfer empanadas, on foil, onto grill over unlit burner. Close lid. Cook for about 20 minutes, rotating foil 180° at halftime, until empanadas are golden brown. Makes 12 empanadas.

***1 empanada:** 220 Calories; 6 g Total Fat (2 g Mono, 0.5 g Poly, 2 g Sat); 10 mg Cholesterol; 35 g Carbohydrate; 2 g Fibre; 7 g Protein; 520 mg Sodium*

VEGAN Vegetable Polenta Skewers

Serve these colourful skewers on a bed of fresh baby spinach for a light repast, or over brown rice for a heartier meal. For best results, do not cut the polenta in advance; it may dry out and be difficult to skewer.

Sweet chili sauce	**1/3 cup**	**75 mL**
Chopped fresh basil (or 3/4 tsp., 4 mL, dried)	**1 tbsp.**	**15 mL**
Small red onion, quartered	**1**	**1**
Polenta roll, cut into 1 inch (2.5 cm) pieces	**1.1 lbs.**	**500 g**
Cherry tomatoes	**12**	**12**
Large pitted green olives	**12**	**12**
Pitted whole black olives	**12**	**12**
Small fresh whole white mushrooms	**12**	**12**
Large green pepper, cut into 12 equal pieces	**1**	**1**
Large red pepper, cut into 12 equal pieces	**1**	**1**
Small zucchini (with peel), cut into 12 slices	**1**	**1**
Bamboo skewers (12 inches, 30 cm, each), soaked in water for 10 minutes	**12**	**12**
Cooking oil	**2 tbsp.**	**30 mL**

Stir chili sauce and basil in small bowl. Set aside.

Peel off top 3 layers in a stack from each onion quarter. Cut each stack lengthwise into 3 equal strips. Save remaining onion for another use.

Thread next 8 ingredients and onion strips alternately onto skewers.

Preheat barbecue to medium. Brush skewers with cooking oil. Place on greased grill. Close lid. Cook for about 12 minutes, turning once, until polenta is heated through and zucchini is tender. Brush with chili sauce mixture. Makes 12 skewers.

***1 skewer:** 100 Calories; 4.5 g Total Fat (2.5 g Mono, 1 g Poly, 0 g Sat); 0 mg Cholesterol; 14 g Carbohydrate; 2 g Fibre; 2 g Protein; 330 mg Sodium*

Pictured on page 125.

Portobello "Steak" Fajitas

Portobello mushrooms have an earthy taste and a meaty texture, making these fajitas sure to please both the vegetarians and the meat-eaters in your life.

Portobello mushrooms, gills and stems removed (see Tip, page 73)	**2**	**2**
Montreal steak spice	**1/2 tsp**	**2 mL**
Medium zucchini (with peel), cut lengthwise into 1/4 inch (6 mm) slices	**1**	**1**
Large red pepper, quartered	**1**	**1**
Large yellow pepper, quartered	**1**	**1**
Lime juice	**1 tbsp.**	**15 mL**
Chili powder	**2 tsp.**	**10 mL**
Salt	**1/8 tsp.**	**0.5 mL**
Flour tortillas (7 1/2 inch, 19 cm, diameter)	**8**	**8**
Sour cream	**1/2 cup**	**125 mL**
Salsa	**1/2 cup**	**125 mL**
Grated Mexican cheese blend	**1 cup**	**250 mL**

Preheat barbecue to medium. Place mushrooms, stem-side down, on greased grill. Close lid. Cook for 5 minutes. Turn over. Sprinkle with steak spice. Close lid. Cook for another 5 minutes until tender. Remove to plate. Cover to keep warm.

Place zucchini, red pepper and yellow pepper on greased grill. Close lid. Cook for about 10 minutes, turning once, until tender. Cut zucchini, peppers and mushrooms into thin strips. Transfer to medium bowl.

Sprinkle with next 3 ingredients. Toss.

Place tortillas on greased grill. Cook for about 30 seconds per side until heated through. Spoon sour cream and salsa down centre of tortillas. Sprinkle with cheese. Top with mushroom mixture. Fold bottom end of tortilla over filling. Fold sides over, leaving top end open. Makes 8 fajitas.

1 fajita: *260 Calories; 10 g Total Fat (2.5 g Mono, 1 g Poly, 5 g Sat); 20 mg Cholesterol; 35 g Carbohydrate; 4 g Fibre; 9 g Protein; 560 mg Sodium*

Pictured on page 144.

Stuffed Summer Squash

Asian eggplant also works well here. Top with Cheese Sauce (page 140), chopped basil and diced red peppers, if desired.

Medium summer squash (green or yellow zucchini)	**6**	**6**
Olive oil	**4 tbsp.**	**60 mL**
Medium red onion, finely chopped	**1**	**1**
Celery stalk, diced	**1**	**1**
Ground cumin	**1 tbsp.**	**15 mL**
Fresh thyme, chopped	**1/2 tbsp.**	**7 mL**
Garlic cloves, minced	**3**	**3**
Tomato paste	**1 tbsp.**	**15 mL**
Medium tomatoes, seeded and diced	**2**	**2**
Large carrot, finely grated	**1**	**1**
Large yam, peeled and diced,	**1**	**1**
Salt	**1 tsp**	**5 mL**
Bay leaf	**1**	**1**
Gruyere cheese, grated	**3/4 cup**	**175 mL**
Fresh basil, chopped	**1 tbsp.**	**15 mL**

Preheat the oven to 400°F (200°C). Slice squash in half. Carefully scoop out flesh, leaving a 1/4 inch (6 mm) ring around squash and keeping outer skin intact. Transfer flesh to cutting board and chop. Set aside.

Heat 2 tbsp. (30 mL) olive oil in large frying pan on medium. Add onions, celery, cumin and thyme. Cook without browning for 2 to 3 minutes, stirring occasionally. Add garlic, tomato paste and tomatoes. Cook for 5 minutes, stirring. Add carrots, yams, squash flesh, bay leaf and salt. Cover and simmer for about 20 minutes, stirring occasionally until vegetables are soft.

Discard bay leaf. Stir in 1/2 cup (125 mL) cheese and 1/2 tbsp. (7 mL) basil. Stuff squash shell with vegetable mixture and sprinkle with remaining cheese and basil. Place squash in casserole dish and drizzle with remaining 2 tbsp. (30 mL) olive oil. Pour 1 cup (250 mL) water on bottom of dish and bake for about 40 to 45 minutes until top is golden. Serves 6.

1 serving: *240 Calories; 14 g Total Fat (8 g Mono, 1.5 g Poly, 4 g Sat); 15 mg Cholesterol; 22 g Carbohydrate; 5 g Fibre; 8 g Protein; 480 mg Sodium*

Pictured on front cover.

Thai Tofu Satay

Tofu with creamy peanut sauce on a bed of grilled suey choy, all tossed in lively Thai dressing.

Medium suey choy (Chinese cabbage), quartered lengthwise (about 2 lbs., 900 g)	**1**	**1**
Package of firm tofu, cut into 3/4 inch (4 cm) cubes	**12.75 oz.**	**350 g**
Bamboo skewers (8 inches, 20 cm, each) soaked in water for 10 minutes	**12**	**12**
Thai peanut sauce	**1/2 cup**	**125 mL**
Soy sauce	**3 tbsp.**	**45 mL**
Brown sugar, packed	**2 tbsp.**	**30 mL**
Lime juice	**2 tbsp.**	**30 mL**
Dried crushed chilies	**1/8 tsp.**	**0.5 mL**
Fresh bean sprouts	**2 cups**	**500 mL**
Grated carrot	**1/2 cup**	**125 mL**
Chopped green onion	**1/2 cup**	**125 mL**
Chopped fresh cilantro	**2 tbsp.**	**30 mL**
Chopped salted peanuts	**1/4 cup**	**60 mL**

Preheat barbecue to medium-high. Place suey choy on greased grill. Close lid. Cook for about 8 minutes, turning often, until browned but still crisp. Remove to cutting board. Slice into 1/4 inch (6 mm) strips. Set aside.

Thread tofu onto skewers. Brush with peanut sauce. Place skewers on greased grill. Close lid. Cook for about 8 minutes, turning at halftime and brushing with remaining peanut sauce, until browned and heated through.

Stir next 4 ingredients in large bowl until sugar is dissolved.

Add next 4 ingredients and suey choy. Toss until coated. Divide cabbage mixture between 6 serving plates. Top each with 2 tofu skewers.

Sprinkle with peanuts. Serves 6.

1 serving: *220 Calories; 12 g Total Fat (2 g Mono, 1.5 g Poly, 2 g Sat); 0 mg Cholesterol; 18 g Carbohydrate; 3 g Fibre; 15 g Protein; 670 mg Sodium*

Hawaiian Pizza Picks

These veggie ham and pineapple sticks would be great to serve at a kid's birthday party or just for a relaxed evening at home.

Can of pineapple chunks, drained	**14 oz.**	**398 mL**
Cubed paneer cheese (about 3/4 inch, 4 cm, pieces)	**16**	**16**
Large red pepper, cut into 16 equal pieces	**1**	**1**
Veggie (meatless) ham slices, folded into quarters (about 4 1/2 oz., 130 g)	**8**	**8**
Bamboo skewers (8 inches, 20 cm each), soaked in water for 10 minutes	**8**	**8**
Pizza sauce	**1/2 cup**	**125 mL**

Preheat barbecue to medium-high. Thread first 4 ingredients onto skewers.

Place skewers on greased grill. Close lid. Cook for about 10 minutes, turning at halftime and brushing with pizza sauce, until browned and heated through. Makes 8 skewers.

1 skewer: *130 Calories; 6 g Total Fat (0 g Mono, 0 g Poly, 3.5 g Sat); 15 mg Cholesterol; 11 g Carbohydrate; 1 g Fibre; 9 g Protein; 220 mg Sodium*

1. Avocado Quinoa Salad, page 38
2. Orzo Black Bean Salad, page 41
3. Apple Fig Pita Salad, page 40

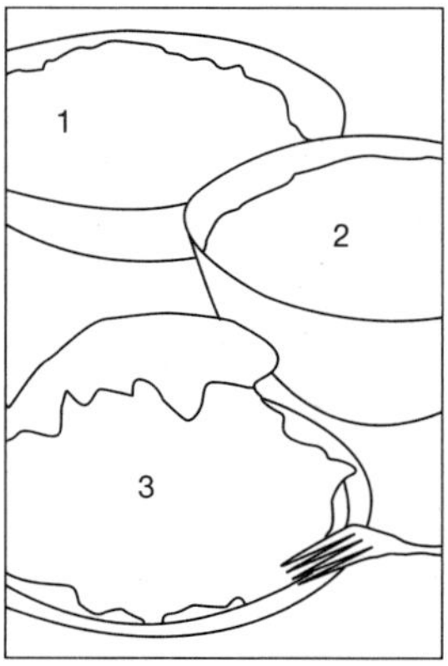

Grilled Stuffed Mushrooms

Mexican-inspired stuffed mushrooms that are quick and easy to get to the table. Serve on a bed of shredded lettuce and provide a variety of toppings such as guacamole, chopped green onions and diced tomatoes to enhance the experience.

Portobello mushrooms, stems and gills removed (see Tip, below)	**4**	**4**
Cooking oil	**2 tbsp.**	**30 mL**
Can of white kidney beans, rinsed and drained, coarsely mashed	**14 oz.**	**398 mL**
Grated jalapeño Monterey Jack cheese	**1 cup**	**250 mL**
Salsa	**1/2 cup**	**125 mL**

Preheat barbecue to medium. Brush mushrooms with cooking oil. Place, stem-side down, on greased grill. Close lid. Cook for about 5 minutes until grill marks appear. Transfer, stem-side up, to large plate.

Combine beans and cheese. Press bean mixture into mushrooms. Place on greased grill, bean mixture–side up. Close lid. Cook for about 5 minutes until filling is heated through and mushrooms are tender.

Spoon salsa over top. Makes 4 stuffed mushrooms.

1 stuffed mushroom: *240 Calories; 14 g Total Fat (4 g Mono, 2 g Poly, 4.5 Sat); 20 mg Cholesterol; 16 g Carbohydrate; 8 g Fibre; 11 g Protein; 620 mg Sodium*

Pictured on page 125.

tip Because the gills can sometimes be bitter, make sure to remove them from the portobellos. Scrape out and discard the gills with a small spoon.

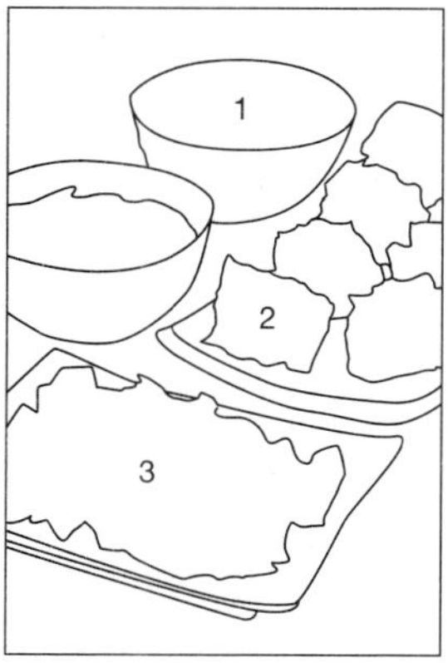

1. Thai Hot and Sour Soup, page 50
2. Sushi Vegetable Squares, page 15
3. Ginger Tofu Stir-Fry, page 115

Grilled Cajun Pizza

Veggie pizza baked in the barbecue over indirect heat then crisped and browned over direct heat for a few minutes.

Prebaked multi-grain (or whole-wheat) pizza crust (12 inch, 30 cm, diameter)	1	1
Tomato sauce	1/2 cup	125 mL
Cajun seasoning	1 tsp.	5 mL
Hot pepper sauce	1 tsp.	5 mL
Chopped fresh oregano (or 1/4 tsp., 1 mL, dried)	1 tsp.	5 mL
Chopped fresh thyme (or 1/8 tsp., 0.5 mL, dried)	1/2 tsp.	2 mL
Diced green pepper	1/2 cup	125 mL
Diced yellow pepper	1/2 cup	125 mL
Diced red onion	1/4 cup	60 mL
Grated Monterey Jack cheese	1 cup	250 mL
Diced tomato	1/2 cup	125 mL

Place crust on sheet of greased heavy-duty (or double layer of regular) foil. Stir next 5 ingredients in small bowl. Spread over crust.

Combine next 3 ingredients in separate small bowl. Scatter over sauce mixture.

Sprinkle with cheese. To preheat barbecue, turn on one burner. Adjust burner to maintain interior barbecue temperature of medium-high. Transfer pizza, on foil, onto grill over unlit burner. Close lid. Cook for 20 minutes, rotating foil 180° at halftime. Move to grill over lit burner. Close lid. Cook for about 3 minutes until crust is browned and crisp.

Sprinkle with tomato. Cuts into 8 wedges.

__1 wedge:__ 140 Calories; 5 g Total Fat (0 g Mono, 0 g Poly, 2.5 g Sat); 10 mg Cholesterol; 18 g Carbohydrate; 2 g Fibre; 7 g Protein; 480 mg Sodium

VEGAN

Summer Mixed Grill

Grill-roasted vegetables over a medley of lentils, tomatoes and olives dressed in a fresh herb vinaigrette.

Olive oil	2 tbsp.	30 mL
Basil pesto	1 tbsp.	15 mL
Baby potatoes, larger ones halved	1/2 lb.	225 g
Bamboo skewers (8 inches, 20 cm, each), soaked in water for 10 minutes	2	2
Medium red onion, quartered	1	1
Small zucchini (with peel), sliced diagonally about 1/2 inch (12 mm) thick	2	2
Large yellow pepper, quartered	1	1
Red wine vinegar	2 tbsp.	30 mL
Olive oil	2 tbsp.	30 mL
Lemon juice	1 tbsp.	15 mL
Finely chopped fresh basil	1 tsp.	5 mL
Chopped fresh oregano	1 tsp.	5 mL
Dijon mustard	1/2 tsp.	2 mL
Salt	1/2 tsp.	2 mL
Pepper	1/4 tsp.	1 mL
Can of lentils, rinsed and drained	19 oz.	540 mL
Halved grape tomatoes	1 cup	250 mL
Sliced black olives	1/4 cup	60 mL

Stir first amount of olive oil and pesto in small cup.

Preheat barbecue to medium. Thread potatoes onto skewers. Arrange potatoes and onion on greased grill. Brush with pesto mixture. Close lid. Cook for about 10 minutes. Turn. Add zucchini and yellow pepper. Brush with pesto mixture. Cook for about 10 minutes, turning at halftime, until potatoes are tender and pepper is tender-crisp. Transfer to cutting board. Slice onion and yellow pepper. Remove potato from skewers.

Whisk next 8 ingredients in large bowl. Add remaining 3 ingredients. Stir. Divide onto 4 plates. Arrange grilled vegetables over lentil mixture. Serves 4.

***1 serving:** 490 Calories; 19 g Total Fat (11 g Mono, 1.5 g Poly, 2.5 g Sat); 0 mg Cholesterol; 72 g Carbohydrate; 12 g Fibre; 16 g Protein; 640 mg Sodium*

Pictured on page 125.

Spanakopita Tart

Appealing spinach pie flavours in a tart form.
Serve with tzatziki and diced tomatoes.

Cooking oil	**1 tsp.**	**5 mL**
Thinly sliced fennel bulb (white part only)	**3/4 cup**	**175 mL**
Thinly sliced red onion	**3/4 cup**	**175 mL**
Garlic clove, minced (or 1/4 tsp., 1 mL, powder)	**1**	**1**
Large eggs, fork-beaten	**2**	**2**
Box of frozen chopped spinach, thawed and squeezed dry	**10 oz.**	**300 mL**
Ricotta cheese	**1 cup**	**250 mL**
Crumbled feta cheese	**1/2 cup**	**125 mL**
Chopped fresh parsley (or 1 1/2 tsp., 7 mL, flakes)	**2 tbsp.**	**30 mL**
Grated lemon zest	**1/4 tsp.**	**1 mL**
Pepper	**1/4 tsp.**	**1 mL**
Package of puff pastry (14 oz., 397 g), thawed according to package directions	**1/2**	**1/2**

Heat cooking oil in medium frying pan on medium. Add fennel and onion. Cook for about 10 minutes, stirring often, until softened.

Add garlic. Heat and stir for about 1 minute until fragrant. Transfer to large bowl. Let stand until cool.

Add next 7 ingredients. Stir.

Roll out pastry on lightly floured surface to 10 x 14 inch (25 x 35 cm) rectangle. Press into bottom and up sides of ungreased 9 x 13 inch (23 x 33 cm) pan. Spread spinach mixture over pastry. Bake on bottom rack in 350°F (175°C) oven for about 35 minutes until set and pastry is puffed and golden. Cuts into 8 pieces.

(continued on next page)

1 piece: 240 Calories; 15 g Total Fat (7 g Mono, 1.5 g Poly, 6 g Sat); 50 mg Cholesterol; 16 g Carbohydrate; 2 g Fibre; 9 g Protein; 270 mg Sodium

Pictured on page 35.

SPANAKOPITA GALETTE: Instead of pressing rolled-out pastry into a 9 x 13 inch (23 x 33 cm) pan, place on an ungreased baking sheet. Spread spinach mixture over pastry, leaving 1 inch (2.5 cm) border on each side. Fold a section of border over spinach. Repeat with next section, allowing pastry to overlap so that a fold is created. Pinch to seal. Repeat until pastry border is completely folded around filling. Bake on bottom rack in 350°F (175°C) oven for about 35 minutes until set and pastry is puffed and golden.

Favourite Roast

A Company's Coming Classic. When you serve this, your guests will think they are eating meatloaf. Use leftovers for sandwiches or a picnic.

Large eggs	**3**	**3**
Cottage cheese	**2 cups**	**500 mL**
Milk	**1/4 cup**	**60 mL**
Liquid gravy browner	**1/2 tsp.**	**2 mL**
Bran flakes cereal	**4 1/2 cups**	**1.1 L**
Finely chopped onion	**1 cup**	**250 mL**
Ground pecans	**1/2 cup**	**125 mL**
Grated sharp Cheddar cheese	**1/3 cup**	**75 mL**
Cooking oil	**1/4 cup**	**60 mL**
Vegetable bouillon powder	**1 tbsp.**	**15 mL**
Ground thyme	**1/4 tsp.**	**1 mL**
Ketchup	**2 tbsp.**	**30 mL**

Beat first 4 ingredients in large bowl.

Add next 7 ingredients. Mix well. Press in greased 9 x 5 x 3 inch (23 x 12 x 7.5 cm) loaf pan.

Spread ketchup over top. Bake in 375°F (190°C) oven for about 45 minutes until set and internal temperature reaches 165°F (74°C). Cuts into 10 slices.

1 slice: 220 Calories; 14 g Total Fat (7 g Mono, 3 g Poly, 3 g Sat); 70 mg Cholesterol; 16 g Carbohydrate; 3 g Fibre; 11 g Protein; 620 mg Sodium

Potluck Baked Beans

A Company's Coming Classic. A bean dish to end all bean dishes. Different and excellent.

Cans of baked beans in tomato sauce (14 oz., 398 mL, each)	**2**	**2**
Can of kidney beans (with liquid)	**14 oz.**	**398 mL**
Can of lima beans, rinsed and drained	**14 oz.**	**398 mL**
Can of mushroom stems and pieces, drained	**10 oz.**	**284 mL**
Cooking oil	**2 tbsp.**	**30 mL**
Chopped onion	**2 1/2 cups**	**625 mL**
Brown sugar, packed	**3/4 cup**	**175 mL**
White vinegar	**1/4 cup**	**60 mL**
Liquid smoke (optional)	**1 tsp.**	**5 mL**

Combine first 4 ingredients in large bowl.

Heat cooking oil in large frying pan on medium. Add onion. Cook for about 10 minutes, stirring often, until softened. Stir into bean mixture.

Add remaining 3 ingredients. Stir well. Transfer to ungreased 3 quart (3 L) casserole. Bake, uncovered, in 325°F (160°C) oven for about 1 hour until thickened. Makes about 10 cups (2.5 L).

***1 cup (250 mL):** 200 Calories; 3 g Total Fat (1.5 g Mono, 1 g Poly, 0 g Sat); 0 mg Cholesterol; 37 g Carbohydrate; 6 g Fibre; 5 g Protein; 300 mg Sodium*

Greek Cannelloni

Flavours of Greece turn an Italian classic into a new favourite. For faster preparation, melted cheese takes the place of béchamel sauce.

Olive oil	2 tsp.	10 mL
Chopped fresh white mushrooms	1 cup	250 mL
Chopped onion	1 cup	250 mL
Diced green pepper	1 cup	250 mL
Can of crushed tomatoes	28 oz.	796 mL
Prepared vegetable broth	1 cup	250 mL
Greek seasoning	2 tsp.	10 mL
Large egg	1	1
Ricotta cheese	1 1/2 cups	375 mL
Box of frozen chopped spinach, thawed and squeezed dry	10 oz.	300 mL
Crumbled feta cheese	3/4 cup	175 mL
Grated lemon zest	2 tsp.	10 mL
Oven-ready cannelloni shells	18	18
Chopped kalamata olives	1/2 cup	125 mL
Grated mozzarella cheese	3/4 cup	175 mL
Crumbled feta cheese	1/2 cup	125 mL

Heat olive oil in large frying pan on medium. Add next 3 ingredients. Cook for about 10 minutes, stirring often, until onion is softened.

Add next 3 ingredients. Stir. Spread half of tomato mixture in greased 9 x 13 inch (23 x 33 cm) baking dish.

Combine next 5 ingredients in medium bowl. Spoon mixture into large resealable freezer bag with piece snipped off corner. Pipe into pasta shells. Arrange in single layer over tomato mixture in baking dish. Pour remaining tomato mixture over top.

Scatter remaining 3 ingredients, in order given, over top. Cover with greased foil. Bake in 350°F (175°C) oven for about 1 hour until pasta is tender. Carefully remove foil. Bake for about 15 minutes until cheese is golden. Let stand for 10 minutes. Makes 18 cannelloni.

1 cannelloni: *140 Calories; 6 g Total Fat (2.5 g Mono, 0 g Poly, 3 g Sat); 25 mg Cholesterol; 13 g Carbohydrate; 2 g Fibre; 8 g Protein; 440 mg Sodium*

Pictured on page 35.

Eight-veggie Lasagna

This colourful lasagna has eight vegetables and a tofu filling. To make the recipe vegan, use soy or rice cheeses and omit the egg.

Cooking oil	**1 tbsp.**	**15 mL**
Chopped carrot	**1 cup**	**250 mL**
Chopped fennel bulb (white part only)	**1 cup**	**250 mL**
Chopped onion	**1 cup**	**250 mL**
Italian seasoning	**1 1/2 tsp.**	**7 mL**
Chopped zucchini (with peel)	**1 1/2 cups**	**375 mL**
Jar of roasted red peppers, drained and chopped	**12 oz.**	**340 mL**
Garlic cloves, minced (or 1/2 tsp., 2 mL, powder)	**2**	**2**
Tomato pasta sauce	**4 cups**	**1 L**
Water	**1 cup**	**250 mL**
Package of firm tofu	**12.75 oz.**	**350 g**
Box of frozen spinach, thawed and squeezed dry	**10 oz.**	**300 g**
Grated Parmesan cheese	**1/4 cup**	**60 mL**
Large egg, fork-beaten	**1**	**1**
Oven-ready lasagna noodles	**12**	**12**
Grated mozzarella cheese	**2 cups**	**500 mL**

Heat cooking oil in large frying pan on medium. Add next 4 ingredients. Cook for about 10 minutes, stirring often, until carrot is softened. Add next 3 ingredients. Cook for about 3 minutes, stirring occasionally, until zucchini is tender-crisp.

Stir pasta sauce and water in medium bowl.

Mash tofu with fork in large bowl until almost smooth. Add next 3 ingredients. Stir.

To assemble, layer ingredients in greased 9 x 13 inch (23 x 33 cm) baking dish as follows:

1. 1 cup (250 mL) sauce mixture
2. 4 noodles

(continued on next page)

3. Zucchini mixture

4. Half of remaining sauce mixture

5. 4 noodles

6. Tofu mixture

7. Remaining noodles

8. Remaining sauce mixture

Sprinkle with mozzarella cheese. Cover with greased foil. Bake in 350°F (175°C) oven for about 1 hour until noodles are tender. Remove foil. Bake for about 20 minutes until cheese is golden. Let stand for 10 minutes. Cuts into 8 pieces.

1 piece: *360 Calories; 12 g Total Fat (2.5 g Mono, 0.5 g Poly, 4 g Sat); 30 mg Cholesterol; 46 g Carbohydrate; 7 g Fibre; 20 g Protein; 840 mg Sodium*

Could-be Chicken Loaf

A Company's Coming Classic. It looks like a chicken loaf and might even fool your guests.

Large eggs	**4**	**4**
Milk	**2 cups**	**500 mL**
Ground sage	**1 tsp.**	**5 mL**
Salt	**2 tsp.**	**10 mL**
Chopped walnuts	**2 cups**	**500 mL**
Fine dry bread crumbs	**2 cups**	**500 mL**

Beat eggs in bowl until frothy. Beat in next 3 ingredients.

Add walnuts and bread crumbs. Stir. Transfer to greased 9 x 5 x 3 inch (23 x 12 x 7.5 cm) loaf pan. Bake, uncovered, in 350°F (175°C) oven for 40 to 45 minutes. Cuts into 10 slices.

1 slice: *280 Calories; 18 g Total Fat (3 g Mono, 12 g Poly, 2.5 g Sat); 55 mg Cholesterol; 22 g Carbohydrate; 3 g Fibre; 10 g Protein; 680 mg Sodium*

Tomato Shepherd's Pie

A traditional-looking shepherd's pie that boasts family-friendly flavours. The veggie ground round works perfectly with the vegetables and mashed potato.

Chopped peeled potato	**4 cups**	**1 L**
Milk	**1/3 cup**	**75 mL**
Butter (or hard margarine)	**2 tbsp.**	**30 mL**
Salt	**1/2 tsp.**	**2 mL**
Cooking oil	**2 tsp.**	**10 mL**
Chopped celery	**1 cup**	**250 mL**
Chopped onion	**1 cup**	**250 mL**
Frozen carrots and peas mix, thawed	**2 cups**	**500 mL**
Package of veggie ground round (see Note)	**12 oz.**	**340 g**
Frozen kernel corn, thawed	**1 cup**	**250 mL**
Can of diced tomatoes (with juice)	**14 oz.**	**398 mL**
Sun-dried tomato pesto	**3 tbsp.**	**45 mL**

Pour water into large saucepan until about 1 inch (2.5 cm) deep. Add potato. Cover. Bring to a boil. Reduce heat to medium. Boil gently for 12 to 15 minutes until tender. Drain. Add next 3 ingredients. Mash.

Heat cooking oil in large frying pan on medium. Add celery and onion. Cook for about 10 minutes, stirring often, until celery is softened.

Add next 5 ingredients. Stir. Transfer to greased 8 x 8 inch (20 x 20 cm) baking dish. Spread mashed potatoes over top. Bake in 375°F (190°C) oven for about 45 minutes until heated through. Serves 4.

__1 serving:__ 440 Calories; 13 g Total Fat (3 g Mono, 1 g Poly, 4.5 g Sat); 15 mg Cholesterol; 62 g Carbohydrate; 10 g Fibre; 25 g Protein; 1220 mg Sodium

Pictured on page 35.

Note: Veggie ground round is available in the produce section of your grocery store.

Three-cheese Fusilli

This enticing pasta casserole with rich cheese sauce is accented with sun-dried tomatoes.

Fusilli pasta	**5 cups**	**1.25 L**
Butter (or hard margarine)	**3 tbsp.**	**45 mL**
Finely chopped green pepper	**1 cup**	**250 mL**
Finely chopped onion	**1 cup**	**250 mL**
Garlic clove, minced (or 1/2 tsp., 2 mL, powder)	**2**	**2**
Salt	**1/4 tsp.**	**1 mL**
Pepper	**1/4 tsp.**	**1 mL**
Ground nutmeg, pinch		
All-purpose flour	**2 tbsp.**	**30 mL**
Milk	**1 1/2 cups**	**375 mL**
Crumbled feta cheese	**3/4 cup**	**175 mL**
Grated Asiago cheese	**1/2 cup**	**125 mL**
Sun-dried tomatoes, softened in boiling water for 10 minutes before chopping	**1/3 cup**	**75 mL**
Fresh bread crumbs (about 1 bread slice)	**1/2 cup**	**125 mL**
Grated Parmesan cheese	**1/4 cup**	**60 mL**

Cook pasta according to package directions. Drain.

Melt butter in large saucepan on medium. Add next 6 ingredients. Cook for about 5 minutes, stirring occasionally, until onion is softened.

Add flour. Heat and stir for 1 minute. Slowly add milk, stirring constantly until smooth. Heat and stir until boiling and thickened.

Add next 3 ingredients. Stir until smooth. Add pasta. Stir. Transfer to greased 2 quart (2 L) casserole.

Combine bread crumbs and Parmesan cheese in small bowl. Sprinkle over pasta mixture. Bake, uncovered, in 375°F (190°C) oven for about 25 minutes until lightly browned. Makes about 7 cups (1.75 L).

1 cup (250 mL): *360 Calories; 14 g Total Fat (2.5 g Mono, 0 g Poly, 8 g Sat); 45 mg Cholesterol; 45 g Carbohydrate; 3 g Fibre; 13 g Protein; 640 mg Sodium*

Walnut Cabbage Bake

A combination of gluten-free grains and light Mediterranean flavours in a rustic tomatoey dish.

Olive (or cooking) oil	1 tsp.	5 mL
Chopped celery	1 cup	250 mL
Chopped onion	1 cup	250 mL
Chopped carrot	1/2 cup	125 mL
Garlic cloves, minced (or 3/4 tsp., 4 mL, powder)	3	3
Prepared vegetable broth	4 cups	1 L
Can of tomato sauce	7 1/2 oz.	213 mL
Chopped walnuts, toasted (see Tip, page 148)	1 cup	250 mL
Long-grain brown rice	1 cup	250 mL
Quinoa, rinsed and drained	1/2 cup	125 mL
Ground allspice	1/2 tsp.	2 mL
Salt	1/4 tsp.	1 mL
Pepper	1/8 tsp.	0.5 mL
Shredded cabbage, lightly packed	5 cups	1.25 L
Chopped tomato	1 1/2 cups	375 mL
Chopped fresh mint	2 tbsp.	30 mL
Lemon juice	1 tbsp.	15 mL

Heat olive oil in large frying pan on medium. Add next 4 ingredients. Cook for about 10 minutes, stirring occasionally, until celery is tender.

Add next 8 ingredients. Heat and stir until boiling. Transfer to greased 9 x 13 inch (23 x 33 cm) baking dish.

Scatter cabbage over rice mixture. Bake, covered, in 350°F (175°C) oven for about 90 minutes, stirring at halftime, until rice is tender. Let stand, covered, for 10 minutes.

Stir in remaining 3 ingredients. Makes about 10 cups (2.5 L).

1 cup (250 mL): *210 Calories; 9 g Total Fat (1.5 g Mono, 5 g Poly, 1 g Sat); 0 mg Cholesterol; 30 g Carbohydrate; 5 g Fibre; 5 g Protein; 440 mg Sodium*

Pictured on page 107.

Dinner Party Pasta Shells

An elegant stuffed pasta dish with no last-minute fuss. Enjoy with a glass of hearty Italian red wine.

Jumbo shell pasta	24	24
Olive oil	1 tsp.	5 mL
Chopped fennel bulb (white part only)	1 cup	250 mL
Chopped onion	1 cup	250 mL
Chopped carrot	1/2 cup	125 mL
Salt	1/4 tsp.	1 mL
Pepper	1/4 tsp.	1 mL
Can of navy beans, rinsed and drained	19 oz.	540 mL
Soft goat (chèvre) cheese	3 1/2 oz.	100 g
Chopped fresh basil	1 tbsp.	15 mL
Dried oregano	1/2 tsp.	2 mL
Tomato sauce	2 cups	500 mL
Fresh bread crumbs	1/2 cup	125 mL
Grated Parmesan cheese	1/2 cup	125 mL
Chopped fresh parsley	1 tbsp.	15 mL

Cook pasta shells according to package directions. Drain.

Heat olive oil in large frying pan on medium. Add next 5 ingredients. Cook for about 15 minutes, stirring occasionally, until vegetables are tender.

Process next 4 ingredients in food processor with on/off motion until just combined. Add vegetable mixture. Process with on/off motion until combined. Spoon into large resealable freezer bag with piece snipped off corner. Pipe into pasta shells.

Spread sauce in bottom of 9 x 13 inch (23 x 33 cm) baking dish. Arrange pasta shells in single layer over sauce. Bake, covered, in 350°F (175°C) oven for about 40 minutes until heated through.

Combine remaining 3 ingredients in small bowl. Sprinkle over shells. Bake, uncovered, for about 15 minutes until topping is golden. Makes 20 shells. Serves 4.

1 serving: *280 Calories; 6 g Total Fat (1.5 g Mono, 0 g Poly, 3.5 g Sat); 15 mg Cholesterol; 42 g Carbohydrate; 7 g Fibre; 13 g Protein; 860 mg Sodium*

Hide and Seek Pasta Bake

An easy and colourful dinner that kids will gobble up. You can use any frozen vegetables that you like, but we like using a carrot, peas and corn mixture—the small veggies hide in the shells!

Small shell pasta	**2 cups**	**500 mL**
Frozen mixed vegetables	**2 cups**	**500 mL**
Can of evaporated milk	**13 oz.**	**370 mL**
Grated sharp Cheddar cheese	**1 cup**	**250 mL**
Large eggs	**3**	**3**
Seasoned salt	**1/2 tsp.**	**2 mL**
Grated sharp Cheddar cheese	**1/2 cup**	**125 mL**

Cook pasta in boiling, salted water in a Dutch oven for 5 minutes, stirring occasionally. Add vegetables. Cook for another 5 minutes until pasta is tender but firm. Drain.

Whisk next 4 ingredients together in large bowl. Add pasta to egg mixture. Stir. Transfer to greased 2 quart (2 L) casserole.

Sprinkle with second amount of cheese. Bake, uncovered, in 350°F (175°C) oven for about 30 minutes until heated through and cheese is golden. Let stand for 5 minutes. Serves 4.

1 serving: *420 Calories; 18 g Total Fat (5 g Mono, 1 g Poly, 10 g Sat); 150 mg Cholesterol; 43 g Carbohydrate; 2 g Fibre; 22 g Protein; 540 mg Sodium*

Mushroom Tourtière

A mushroom and barley filling takes the place of the traditional meat pie, with truly excellent results. A food processor makes chopping the mushrooms and onion a snap.

TOURTIÈRE FILLING

Pot barley	**1/3 cup**	**75 mL**
Cooking oil	**1 tbsp.**	**15 mL**
Finely chopped fresh white mushrooms	**2 lbs.**	**900 g**

(continued on next page)

Finely chopped onion	1 cup	250 mL
Salt	1 tsp.	5 mL
Pepper	1/4 tsp.	1 mL
Ground allspice	1 tsp.	5 mL
Ground cloves, pinch		

SPICED PASTRY		
All-purpose flour	2 1/2 cups	625 mL
Ground allspice	1/4 tsp.	1 mL
Salt	1/4 tsp.	1 mL
Cayenne pepper	1/8 tsp.	0.5 mL
Cold vegetable shortening, cut up	3/4 cup	175 mL
Cold water	1/3–1/2 cup	75–125 mL

Tourtière Filling: Cook barley in boiling, salted water for about 35 minutes until tender. Drain.

Heat cooking oil in large frying pan on medium-high. Add next 6 ingredients. Cook for about 15 minutes, stirring occasionally, until mixture is browned and liquid is almost evaporated. Add barley. Stir. Transfer to large bowl. Let stand until cooled to room temperature. Makes about 3 2/3 cups (900 mL) filling.

Spiced Pastry: Combine first 4 ingredients in large bowl. Cut in shortening until mixture resembles coarse crumbs. Slowly add water, stirring with fork until mixture starts to come together. Do not overmix. Turn out pastry onto work surface. Shape into slightly flattened disc. Wrap with plastic wrap. Chill for 30 minutes. Divide pastry into 2 portions, making 1 portion slightly larger than the other. Roll out larger portion on lightly floured surface to about 1/8 inch (3 mm) thickness. Line 9 inch (23 cm) pie plate. Fill pie shell with Tourtière Filling. Roll remaining pastry on lightly floured surface to about 1/8 inch (3 mm) thickness. Dampen edge of pie shell with water. Cover with remaining pastry. Trim and crimp decorative edge to seal. Cut several small vents in top of pastry to allow steam to escape. Bake on bottom rack in 425°F (220°C) oven for 15 minutes. Reduce heat to 375°F (190°C). Bake for about 50 minutes until pastry is golden. Let stand for 10 minutes. Cuts into 8 wedges.

1 wedge: *410 Calories; 21 g Total Fat (1 g Mono, 1 g Poly, 4.5 Sat); 0 mg Cholesterol; 48 g Carbohydrate; 4 g Fibre; 9 g Protein; 370 mg Sodium*

Fantasy Meatballs

A Company's Coming Classic.
The fantasy is that it's really hard to tell it isn't meat.

Large eggs	5	5
2% cottage cheese	1 cup	250 mL
Dried basil	1 tsp.	5 mL
Salt	3/4 tsp.	4 mL
Pepper	1/8 tsp.	0.5 mL
Fine dry bread crumbs	2 cups	500 mL
Grated mozzarella cheese	1 cup	250 mL
Ground walnuts	1 cup	250 mL
Chopped onion	3/4 cup	175 mL
Parsley flakes	1 tsp.	5 mL
Poultry seasoning	1 1/4 tsp.	6 mL
Can of tomato sauce	7 1/2 oz.	213 mL
Water	1 cup	250 mL
Granulated sugar	1/2 tsp.	2 mL

Beat first 5 ingredients in large bowl until well combined.

Add next 6 ingredients. Mix well. Let stand for 10 minutes. Shape into 1 1/2 inch (4 cm) balls. Arrange in ungreased 9 x 13 inch (22 x 33 cm) pan in single layer.

Stir remaining 3 ingredients in small bowl. Pour over balls. Bake in 350°F (175°C) oven for about 35 minutes. Makes about 3 dozen meatballs. Serves 8.

1 serving: *320 Calories; 17 g Total Fat (3.5 g Mono, 8 g Poly, 4 g Sat); 100 mg Cholesterol; 26 g Carbohydrate; 3 g Fibre; 16 g Protein; 800 mg Sodium*

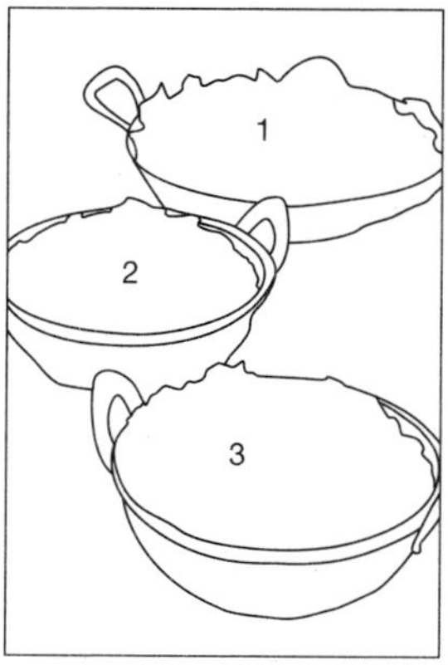

1. Green Bean Green Curry, page 116
2. Biriyani, page 114
3. Chickpea Paneer Curry, page 100

Teriyaki Tofu

A tangy pineapple and teriyaki topping make this a good introduction for tofu novices. Serve over rice with a colourful medley of stir-fried veggies.

Package of firm tofu, cut crosswise into 8 slices	**12.75 oz.**	**350 g**
Thick teriyaki basting sauce	**1/4 cup**	**60 mL**
Canned pineapple slices, drained and halved	**4**	**4**
Sliced green onion	**2 tbsp.**	**30 mL**
Finely chopped red pepper	**2 tbsp.**	**30 mL**

Arrange tofu slices in single layer on greased foil-lined baking sheet. Brush with half of teriyaki sauce. Turn. Brush with remaining sauce. Broil on top rack in oven for about 5 minutes per side until edges are browned.

Arrange pineapple over tofu. Broil for 3 minutes.

Sprinkle with green onion and red pepper. Makes 8 slices.

1 slice: *80 Calories; 3 g Total Fat (0 g Mono, 0 g Poly, 0.5 g Sat); 0 mg Cholesterol; 7 g Carbohydrate; 0 g Fibre; 6 g Protein; 150 mg Sodium*

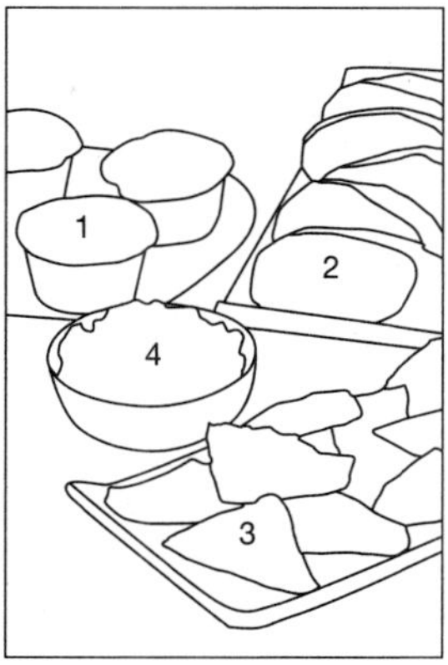

1. Lemon Coconut Cupcakes, page 150
2. Apple Nut Roll-ups, page 149
3. Sesame Super Bars, page 142
4. Sweet and Spicy Edamame, page 141

Caramelized Onion Strudel

Golden phyllo wrapped around a Greek-inspired filling of caramelized onions, spinach, chickpeas, red pepper and olives.

Olive oil	2 tbsp.	30 mL
Chopped onion	6 cups	1.5 L
Salt	1/4 tsp.	1 mL
Pepper	1/4 tsp.	1 mL
Chopped fresh spinach leaves, lightly packed	4 cups	1 L
Can of chickpeas (garbanzo beans), rinsed and drained, coarsely chopped	19 oz.	540 mL
Chopped red pepper	1 cup	250 mL
Chopped kalamata olives	1/4 cup	60 mL
Pine nuts, toasted (see Tip, page 148)	1/4 cup	60 mL
Greek seasoning	1 tbsp.	15 mL
Lemon juice	1 tbsp.	15 mL
Grated lemon zest (see Tip, page 33)	1 tsp.	5 mL
Phyllo pastry sheets, thawed according to package directions	6	6
Olive oil	2 tbsp.	30 mL

Heat first amount of olive oil in large frying pan on medium. Add next 3 ingredients. Stir. Cook, covered, for about 10 minutes until onion is softened. Cook, uncovered, for about 15 minutes, stirring occasionally, until onion is caramelized.

Add next 8 ingredients. Heat and stir until spinach is wilted.

Layer pastry sheets, brushing each layer with second amount of olive oil. Spoon onion mixture along short end, leaving 4 inch (10 cm) edge. Fold edge over filling. Roll up tightly to enclose filling, leaving ends open. Arrange seam-side down on greased baking sheet with sides. Brush with olive oil. Cut several small vents in top to allow steam to escape. Bake in 375°F (190°C) oven for about 35 minutes until golden brown and crisp. Cuts into eight 1 1/2 inch (4 cm) slices.

***1 slice:** 290 Calories; 12 g Total Fat (7 g Mono, 2.5 g Poly, 1.5 g Sat); 0 mg Cholesterol; 38 g Carbohydrate; 7 g Fibre; 10 g Protein; 490 mg Sodium*

Vegetable Coconut Curry

VEGAN

A baked vegetable and rice dish. Butternut squash has an inherent sweetness that nicely complements Thai curry flavours.

Prepared vegetable broth	1 cup	250 mL
Thai red curry paste	2 tbsp.	30 mL
Lemon grass paste (or 1 tbsp., 15 mL, finely chopped lemon grass, bulb only)	1 tbsp.	15 mL
Finely grated ginger root (or 1/2 tsp., 2 mL, ground)	2 tsp.	10 mL
Brown sugar, packed	1 tsp.	5 mL
Garlic cloves, minced	2	2
Chopped butternut squash (see Tip, below)	4 cups	1 L
Frozen shelled edamame (soybeans), thawed	2 cups	500 mL
Can of coconut milk	14 oz.	398 mL
Brown basmati rice	1 cup	250 mL
Chopped onion	1 cup	250 mL
Chopped red pepper	1 cup	250 mL
Chopped fresh spinach leaves, lightly packed	1 1/2 cups	375 mL
Lime juice	2 tbsp.	30 mL
Chopped unsalted, roasted cashews	1/4 cup	60 mL

Whisk first 6 ingredients in large bowl until smooth. Add next 6 ingredients. Stir. Transfer to greased 9 x 13 inch (23 x 33 cm) baking dish. Bake, covered, in 375°F (190°C) oven for about 90 minutes, stirring at halftime, until rice is tender and liquid is absorbed. Let stand for 10 minutes.

Add remaining 3 ingredients. Stir until spinach is wilted. Makes about 6 cups (1.5 L).

1 cup (250 mL): *430 Calories; 21 g Total Fat (0.5 g Mono, 0 g Poly, 13 g Sat); 0 mg Cholesterol; 53 g Carbohydrate; 6 g Fibre; 12 g Protein; 370 mg Sodium*

tip Some people have an allergic reaction to raw squash flesh, so wear rubber gloves when cutting or handling raw butternut squash or acorn squash.

Almost Everything Pizza

A quick-to-assemble pizza that's loaded with delicious toppings.

Prebaked multi-grain (or whole-wheat) pizza crust (12 inch, 30 cm, diameter)	**1**	**1**
Pizza sauce	**1/2 cup**	**125 mL**
Veggie (meatless) pepperoni slices	**3 oz.**	**85 mL**
Grated Italian cheese blend	**1 cup**	**250 mL**
Sliced black olives	**3 tbsp.**	**45 mL**
Sliced green pepper	**1/2 cup**	**125 mL**
Thinly sliced red onion	**1/3 cup**	**75 mL**
Diced tomato	**1/4 cup**	**60 mL**
Chopped fresh basil	**1 tbsp.**	**15 mL**

Place pizza crust on greased 12 inch (30 cm) pizza pan. Spread pizza sauce over crust.

Scatter next 5 ingredients, in order given, over top. Bake in 475°F (240°C) oven for about 15 minutes until crust is crisp and golden and cheese is starting to brown.

Sprinkle with tomato and basil. Cuts into 8 wedges.

__1 wedge:__ 160 Calories; 5 g Total Fat (0 g Mono, 0 g Poly, 1.5 g Sat); 10 mg Cholesterol; 19 g Carbohydrate; 2 g Fibre; 10 g Protein; 470 mg Sodium

Smoky Cheese Potato Bake

A dressed-up potato scallop with layers of cheese, spinach and red pepper. Serve with a leafy green salad.

Ricotta cheese	**2 cups**	**500 mL**
Garlic cloves, minced (or 1/2 tsp., 2 mL, powder)	**2**	**2**
All-purpose flour	**1/4 cup**	**60 mL**
Salt	**1/4 tsp.**	**1 mL**
Pepper	**1/4 tsp.**	**1 mL**

(continued on next page)

Grated smoked Cheddar cheese	**1 1/2 cups**	**375 mL**
Finely chopped roasted red pepper	**1 cup**	**250 mL**
Box of frozen chopped spinach, thawed and squeezed dry	**10 oz.**	**300 mL**
Large eggs	**5**	**5**
Milk	**1/2 cup**	**125 mL**
Grated Parmesan cheese	**1/4 cup**	**60 mL**
Dijon mustard	**1 tsp.**	**5 mL**
Thinly sliced peeled baking potato (about 1/8 inch, 3 mm, thick)	**5 cups**	**1.25 L**

Stir first 5 ingredients in large bowl.

Add next 3 ingredients. Stir well.

Whisk next 4 ingredients in small bowl. To assemble, layer ingredients in well-greased 3 quart (3 L) casserole as follows:

1. 1/3 potato slices
2. Half of ricotta cheese mixture
3. 1/3 potato slices
4. Half of egg mixture
5. Remaining ricotta cheese mixture
6. Remaining potato slices
7. Remaining egg mixture

Bake, covered, in 350°F (175°C) oven for about 75 minutes until potato is tender. Bake, uncovered, for about 15 minutes until golden. Let stand for 10 minutes. Serves 8.

***1 serving:** 210 Calories; 13 g Total Fat (2.5 g Mono, 0.5 g Poly, 7 g Sat); 120 mg Cholesterol; 17 g Carbohydrate; 1 g Fibre; 16 g Protein; 370 mg Sodium*

Spring Vegetable Cobbler

Golden biscuits top a savoury vegetable filling in a herbed sauce.

Cooking oil	2 tsp.	10 mL
Sliced leek (white part only)	4 cups	1 L
Chopped fennel bulb (white part only)	2 cups	500 mL
Dried rosemary, crushed	3/4 tsp.	4 mL
All-purpose flour	2 tbsp.	30 mL
Salt	1/2 tsp.	2 mL
Pepper	1/4 tsp.	1 mL
Chopped fresh asparagus	2 cups	500 mL
Frozen peas	1 1/2 cups	375 mL
Prepared vegetable broth	1 1/2 cups	375 mL
Dijon mustard	1 tbsp.	15 mL
All-purpose flour	1 1/3 cups	325 mL
Baking powder	1 tbsp.	15 mL
Dried basil	1 tsp.	5 mL
Dried dillweed	1 tsp.	5 mL
Salt	1/4 tsp.	1 mL
Cold butter (or hard margarine), cut up	1/4 cup	60 mL
2% cottage cheese	1 cup	250 mL
Water	1/2 cup	125 mL

Heat cooking oil in large frying pan on medium. Add next 3 ingredients. Cook for about 15 minutes, stirring occasionally, until leek is softened. Add next 3 ingredients. Heat and stir for 2 minutes.

Add next 4 ingredients. Cook for about 5 minutes, stirring often, until heated through. Transfer to greased 8 x 8 inch (20 x 20 cm) baking dish.

Combine next 5 ingredients in medium bowl. Cut in butter until mixture resembles coarse crumbs.

Add cottage cheese and water. Stir until just moistened. Drop by mounded tablespoonfuls over hot leek mixture. Bake in 400°F (200°C) oven for about 30 minutes until wooden pick inserted in centre of biscuit comes out clean. Serves 6.

1 serving: *300 Calories; 11 g Total Fat (3 g Mono, 1 g Poly, 6 g Sat); 25 mg Cholesterol; 38 g Carbohydrate; 6 g Fibre; 13 g Protein; 890 mg Sodium*

VEGAN

Megadarra

Megadarra (pronounced me-ga-DAR-ra)—also known as mujadarah (mu-jah-DRA)—is a rich-textured Middle Eastern dish of lentils, brown rice and onions. Olive oil is used in this dish for authentic flavour. Serve with plain Balkan-style yogurt.

Prepared vegetable broth	**5 cups**	**1.25 L**
Dried green lentils	**1 cup**	**250 mL**
Long-grain brown rice	**1 cup**	**250 mL**
Coarsely ground pepper	**3/4 tsp.**	**4 mL**
Ground coriander	**3/4 tsp.**	**4 mL**
Garlic cloves, minced (or 1/2 tsp., 2 mL, powder)	**2**	**2**
Ground allspice	**1/8 tsp.**	**0.5 mL**
Olive oil	**1 tbsp.**	**15 mL**
Thinly sliced onion	**2 1/2 cups**	**625 mL**
Balsamic vinegar	**1 tbsp.**	**15 mL**
Liquid honey	**1 tsp.**	**5 mL**
Salt	**1/4 tsp.**	**1 mL**

Combine first 7 ingredients in well-greased 3 1/2 to 4 quart (3.5 to 4 L) slow cooker. Cook, covered, on Low for 5 to 6 hours or on High for 2 1/2 to 3 hours.

Heat olive oil in large frying pan on medium. Add onion. Cook for about 20 minutes, stirring occasionally, until browned and starting to crisp.

Add remaining 3 ingredients. Stir. Transfer lentil mixture to serving dish. Scatter onion mixture over top. Makes about 6 cups (1.5 L).

__1 cup (250 mL):__ 210 Calories; 3.5 g Total Fat (1.5 g Mono, 0 g Poly, 0 g Sat); 0 mg Cholesterol; 42 g Carbohydrate; 5 g Fibre; 5 g Protein; 610 mg Sodium

Dark Bean Chili

Black beans, mushrooms and onions sautéed until well-browned make this a darker-than-usual chili.

Cooking oil	2 tbsp.	30 mL
Fresh brown (or white) mushrooms, quartered	2 lbs.	900 g
Chopped onion	1 1/2 cups	375 mL
Dry (or alcohol-free) red wine	1 cup	250 mL
Cans of black beans (19 oz., 540 mL, each), rinsed and drained	2	2
Can of crushed tomatoes	28 oz.	796 mL
Can of red kidney beans, rinsed and drained	14 oz.	398 mL
Water	1 1/2 cups	375 mL
Tomato paste	1/4 cup	60 mL
Dried oregano	1 1/2 tsp.	7 mL
Ground cumin	1 1/2 tsp.	7 mL
Granulated sugar	1 tsp.	5 mL
Salt	3/4 tsp.	4 mL
Ground chipotle pepper (or 1/4 tsp., 1 mL, cayenne pepper)	1/2 tsp.	2 mL
Chopped fresh cilantro (or parsley)	1/3 cup	75 mL
Steak sauce	1/4 cup	60 mL

Heat cooking oil in a Dutch oven on medium-high. Add mushrooms and onion. Cook for about 15 minutes, stirring often, until mushrooms are browned and onion is softened. Reduce heat to medium. Add wine. Simmer for 5 minutes. Transfer to 3 1/2 to 4 quart (3.5 to 4 L) slow cooker.

Add next 10 ingredients. Stir. Cook, covered, on Low for 8 to 9 hours or on High for 4 to 4 1/2 hours.

Stir in cilantro and steak sauce. Makes about 11 cups (2.75 L).

1 cup (250 mL): *160 Calories; 3 g Total Fat (1.5 g Mono, 0.5 g Poly, 0 g Sat); 0 mg Cholesterol; 23 g Carbohydrate; 7 g Fibre; 8 g Protein; 510 mg Sodium*

Spanish Stuffed Peppers

VEGAN

These bright bell peppers, stuffed with spicy Spanish flavours, make an attractive main dish. Garnish with chopped fresh parsley for additional colour.

Large red peppers (or your choice of colour)	**4**	**4**
Olive (or cooking) oil	**1 tsp.**	**5 mL**
Chopped onion	**1 cup**	**250 mL**
Garlic cloves, minced	**2**	**2**
Smoked (sweet) paprika	**1 tsp.**	**5 mL**
Cayenne pepper	**1/8 tsp.**	**0.5 mL**
Salt	**1/4 tsp.**	**1 mL**
Can of tomato sauce	**7 1/2 oz.**	**213 mL**
Can of chickpeas (garbanzo beans), rinsed and drained	**19 oz.**	**540 mL**
Cooked long-grain brown rice (about 1/2 cup, 125 mL, uncooked)	**1 1/2 cups**	**375 mL**
Green olives, sliced	**1/2 cup**	**125 mL**
Slivered almonds, toasted (see Tip, page 148)	**1/2 cup**	**125 mL**
Water	**1 cup**	**250 mL**

Cut 1/2 inch (12 mm) from top of each pepper. Remove seeds and ribs. Trim bottom of each pepper so it will sit flat, being careful not to cut into cavity. Set aside. Discard stems from tops, dicing remaining pepper surrounding stem.

Heat olive oil in large frying pan on medium. Add onion and diced pepper. Cook for about 10 minutes, stirring often, until onion is softened. Add next 4 ingredients. Heat and stir for about 1 minute until fragrant.

Add tomato sauce. Bring to a boil, stirring occasionally. Transfer to large bowl.

Add next 4 ingredients. Stir. Spoon into prepared peppers. Arrange upright in 5 to 7 quart (5 to 7 L) slow cooker.

Pour water around stuffed peppers. Cook, covered, on Low for 4 to 5 hours or on High for 2 to 2 1/2 hours. Makes 4 stuffed peppers.

1 stuffed pepper: *450 Calories; 15 g Total Fat (8 g Mono, 3 g Poly, 1.5 g Sat); 0 mg Cholesterol; 67 g Carbohydrate; 17 g Fibre; 18 g Protein; 990 mg Sodium*

Pictured on page 54.

Chickpea Paneer Curry

A mild Indian vegetable curry accompanied by soft cubes of paneer. Serve with naan bread and yogurt.

Cooking oil	**1 tbsp.**	**15 mL**
Sliced onion	**2 cups**	**500 mL**
Mild curry paste	**2 tsp.**	**10 mL**
Garlic clove, minced (or 1/4 tsp., 1 mL, powder)	**1**	**1**
Prepared vegetable broth	**1 1/2 cups**	**375 mL**
Brown sugar, packed	**2 tsp.**	**10 mL**
Can of chickpeas (garbanzo beans), rinsed and drained	**19 oz.**	**540 mL**
Cauliflower florets	**2 cups**	**500 mL**
Sliced carrot	**1 1/2 cups**	**375 mL**
Water	**1 tbsp.**	**15 mL**
Cornstarch	**2 tsp.**	**10 mL**
Chopped fresh spinach leaves, lightly packed	**2 cups**	**500 mL**
Cubed paneer cheese	**1 1/2 cups**	**375 mL**
Frozen peas, thawed	**1 cup**	**250 mL**

Heat cooking oil in large frying pan on medium. Add onion. Cook for about 8 minutes, stirring often, until softened. Add curry paste and garlic. Heat and stir for about 1 minute until fragrant.

Add broth and brown sugar. Heat and stir, scraping any brown bits from bottom of pan, until boiling. Transfer to 3 1/2 to 4 quart (3.5 to 4 L) slow cooker.

Add next 3 ingredients. Stir. Cook, covered, on Low for 4 to 5 hours or on High for 2 to 2 1/2 hours.

Stir water into cornstarch in small cup until smooth. Add to slow cooker.

Add remaining 3 ingredients. Stir. Cook, covered, on High for about 15 minutes until boiling and thickened. Makes about 7 cups (1.75 L).

1 cup (250 mL): *270 Calories; 11 g Total Fat (1 g Mono, 0.5 g Poly, 5 g Sat); 25 mg Cholesterol; 31 g Carbohydrate; 8 g Fibre; 15 g Protein; 370 mg Sodium*

Pictured on page 89.

VEGAN

Tempting Tagine

Serve this hearty Moroccan stew over whole-wheat couscous or, for a gluten-free version, over quinoa.

Sliced carrot (3/4 inch, 2 cm, pieces)	2 cups	500 mL
Sliced parsnip (3/4 inch, 2 cm, pieces)	2 cups	500 mL
Cubed peeled potato (1/2 inch, 12 mm, pieces)	2 cups	500 mL
Cubed peeled orange-fleshed sweet potato (1 inch, 2.5 cm, pieces)	2 cups	500 mL
Cans of chickpeas (garbanzo beans), 19 oz., 540 mL, each, rinsed and drained	2	2
Pitted prunes, halved	1 cup	250 mL
Dried apricots, quartered	1/2 cup	125 mL
Can of diced tomatoes (with juice)	28 oz.	796 mL
Can of crushed tomatoes	14 oz.	398 mL
Garlic cloves, minced (or 3/4 tsp., 4 mL, powder)	3	3
Ground cumin	2 tsp.	10 mL
Ground cinnamon	1/2 tsp.	2 mL
Dried crushed chilies	1/4 tsp.	1 mL
Salt	1/4 tsp.	1 mL
Pepper	1/4 tsp.	1 mL
Chopped fresh parsley	1/4 cup	60 mL

Place first 7 ingredients, in order given, in 5 to 7 quart (5 to 7 L) slow cooker.

Stir next 8 ingredients in large bowl. Stir. Pour over carrot mixture. Do not stir. Cook, covered, on Low for 8 to 9 hours or on High for 4 to 4 1/2 hours.

Add parsley. Stir. Makes about 12 cups (3 L).

1 cup (250 mL): *190 Calories; 1 g Total Fat (0 g Mono, 0 g Poly, 0 g Sat); 0 mg Cholesterol; 41 g Carbohydrate; 8 g Fibre; 6 g Protein; 430 mg Sodium*

VEGAN

Dressed-up Dal

Rich and satisfying. Garnish individual servings with additional chopped tomato and fresh cilantro leaves. Traditionally served with roti or naan bread.

Cooking oil	1 tbsp.	15 mL
Chopped onion	2 cups	500 mL
Garlic cloves, minced (or 3/4 tsp., 4 mL, powder)	3	3
Curry powder	2 tsp.	10 mL
Cumin seed	1 tsp.	5 mL
Brown sugar, packed	1 tsp.	5 mL
Dried crushed chilies	1/4 tsp.	1 mL
Water	6 cups	1.5 L
Dried green lentils	1 cup	250 mL
Dried red spilt lentils	1 cup	250 mL
Cinnamon stick (4 inches, 10 cm)	1	1
Bay leaf	1	1
Chopped fresh spinach leaves, lightly packed	3 cups	750 mL
Chopped tomato	1 cup	250 mL
Chopped fresh cilantro (or parsley)	1/4 cup	60 mL
Lemon juice	3 tbsp.	45 mL
Finely grated ginger root (or 3/4 tsp., 4 mL, ground)	1 tbsp.	15 mL
Salt	1/2 tsp.	2 mL

Heat cooking oil in large frying pan on medium-high. Add onion. Cook for 5 minutes, stirring often, until onion starts to brown.

Add next 5 ingredients. Heat and stir for about 1 minute until fragrant. Transfer to 3 1/2 to 4 quart (3.5 to 4 L) slow cooker.

Add next 5 ingredients. Stir. Cook, covered, on Low for 7 to 8 hours or on High for 3 1/2 to 4 hours.

Discard cinnamon stick and bay leaf. Add remaining 6 ingredients. Stir until spinach is wilted. Makes about 8 cups (2 L).

__1 cup (250 mL):__ 210 Calories; 3 g Total Fat (1 g Mono, 0.5 g Poly, 0 g Sat); 0 mg Cholesterol; 35 g Carbohydrate; 9 g Fibre; 13 g Protein; 170 mg Sodium

Lasagna Fagiole

Romano beans offer this lasagna a smooth and creamy texture, and a short list of ingredients makes it so easy to assemble.

Cooking oil	**2 tsp.**	**10 mL**
Chopped onion	**2 cups**	**250 mL**
Pepper	**1/4 tsp.**	**1 mL**
Tomato garlic pasta sauce	**3 1/2 cups**	**875 mL**
Can of romano beans, rinsed and drained	**19 oz.**	**540 mL**
Water	**1 cup**	**250 mL**
Oven-ready lasagna noodles, broken in half	**9**	**9**
Grated mozzarella cheese	**2 cups**	**500 mL**

Heat cooking oil in large frying pan on medium. Add onion. Sprinkle with pepper. Cook for about 10 minutes, stirring often, until onion is softened.

Add next 3 ingredients. Stir. Remove from heat.

Layer ingredients in greased 5 to 7 quart (5 to 7 L) slow cooker as follows:

1. 1/4 bean mixture
2. 6 noodle halves
3. 1/4 bean mixture
4. 1 cup (250 mL) cheese
5. 6 noodle halves
6. 1/4 bean mixture
7. Remaining noodle halves
8. Remaining bean mixture
9. Remaining cheese

Cook, covered, on Low for 4 to 5 hours or on High for 2 to 2 1/2 hours. Let stand, uncovered, for 10 minutes. Serves 6.

***1 serving:** 370 Calories; 12 g Total Fat (3 g Mono, 0.5 g Poly, 4.5 g Sat); 25 mg Cholesterol; 51 g Carbohydrate; 7 g Fibre; 16 g Protein; 680 mg Sodium*

Jazzy Quinoa Jambalaya

Head to New Orleans for dinner tonight with this healthy one-dish meal. Quinoa replaces the rice of a conventional jambalaya. Serve with hot sauce if you'd like to dial up the heat.

Cooking oil	**1 tbsp.**	**15 mL**
Chopped green pepper	**1 1/2 cups**	**375 mL**
Chopped onion	**1 1/2 cups**	**375 mL**
Chopped celery	**1 cup**	**250 mL**
Garlic cloves, minced (or 3/4 tsp., 4 mL, powder)	**3**	**3**
Tomato paste (see Tip, below)	**2 tbsp.**	**30 mL**
Cajun seasoning	**1 tbsp.**	**15 mL**
Can of diced tomatoes (with juice)	**14 oz.**	**398 mL**
Quinoa, rinsed and drained	**1 1/2 cups**	**375 mL**
Can of red kidney beans, rinsed and drained	**19 oz.**	**540 mL**
Prepared vegetable broth	**2 1/2 cups**	**625 mL**
Chopped red pepper	**1 cup**	**250 mL**
Chopped green onion	**1/2 cup**	**125 mL**

Heat cooking oil in large frying pan on medium. Add next 3 ingredients. Cook for about 10 minutes until celery is softened.

Add next 3 ingredients. Heat and stir for 1 minute. Add tomatoes with juice. Heat and stir until boiling. Transfer to ungreased 3 1/2 to 4 quart (3.5 to 4 L) slow cooker.

Add next 4 ingredients. Stir. Cook, covered, on Low for 5 to 6 hours or on High for 2 1/2 to 3 hours. Stir in green onion. Makes about 9 1/4 cups (2.3 L).

1 cup (250 mL): *170 Calories; 3 g Total Fat (1 g Mono, 0 g Poly, 0 g Sat); 0 mg Cholesterol; 30 g Carbohydrate; 7 g Fibre; 7 g Protein; 740 mg Sodium*

tip If you need less than an entire can of tomato paste, freeze the unopened can for 30 minutes. Open both ends and push the contents through one end. Slice off only what you need. Freeze the remaining paste in a resealable freezer bag or plastic wrap for future use.

Caribbean Vegetable Rice

Coconut rice and tender vegetables with flavours reminiscent of jerk seasoning. Pumpkin seeds add an interesting final touch.

Chopped peeled orange-fleshed sweet potato (about 3/4 inch, 2 cm, pieces)	**4 cups**	**1 L**
Chopped cauliflower	**3 cups**	**750 mL**
Chopped yellow pepper (3/4 inch, 2 cm, pieces)	**2 cups**	**500 mL**
Chopped onion	**1 cup**	**250 mL**
Long-grain brown rice	**1 cup**	**250 mL**
Can of coconut milk	**14 oz.**	**398 mL**
Prepared vegetable broth	**1 cup**	**250 mL**
Brown sugar, packed	**1 tbsp.**	**15 mL**
Chili paste (sambal oelek)	**1 tbsp.**	**15 mL**
Finely grated ginger root (or 1/2 tsp., 2 mL, ground ginger)	**2 tsp.**	**10 mL**
Garlic cloves, minced (or 1/2 tsp., 2 mL, powder)	**2**	**2**
Dried thyme	**1/2 tsp.**	**2 mL**
Ground allspice	**1/2 tsp.**	**2 mL**
Ground cinnamon	**1/4 tsp.**	**1 mL**
Salt	**1/2 tsp.**	**2 mL**
Pepper	**1/4 tsp.**	**1 mL**
Chopped unsalted toasted pumpkin seeds	**1/3 cup**	**75 mL**

Combine first 5 ingredients in greased 3 1/2 to 4 quart (3.5 to 4 L) slow cooker.

Whisk next 11 ingredients in medium bowl. Pour over vegetables. Stir. Cook, covered, on Low for 8 to 9 hours or on High for 4 to 4 1/2 hours.

Sprinkle with pumpkin seeds. Makes about 8 cups (2 L).

1 cup (250 mL): *280 Calories; 11 g Total Fat (0 g Mono, 0 g Poly, 9 g Sat); 0 mg Cholesterol; 42 g Carbohydrate; 5 g Fibre; 5 g Protein; 320 mg Sodium*

Pictured on page 54.

Wild for Ratatouille

Tender, nutty wild rice transforms ratatouille into a complete meal.

Can of diced tomatoes (with juice)	**28 oz.**	**796 mL**
Chopped peeled eggplant (1 inch, 2.5 cm, pieces)	**3 cups**	**750 mL**
Chopped yellow pepper	**2 cups**	**500 mL**
Chopped zucchini (with peel), 1 inch (2.5 cm) pieces	**2 cups**	**500 mL**
Prepared vegetable broth	**2 cups**	**500 mL**
Can of crushed tomatoes	**14 oz.**	**398 mL**
Chopped onion	**1 1/2 cups**	**375 mL**
Chopped celery	**1 cup**	**250 mL**
Wild rice	**1 cup**	**250 mL**
Garlic cloves, minced (or 1/2 tsp., 2 mL, powder)	**2**	**2**
Granulated sugar	**1 tsp.**	**5 mL**
Italian seasoning	**1 tsp.**	**5 mL**
Salt	**1/4 tsp.**	**1 mL**
Pepper	**1/4 tsp.**	**1 mL**
Chopped fresh parsley	**3 tbsp.**	**45 mL**

Combine first 14 ingredients in greased 4 to 5 quart (4 to 5 L) slow cooker. Cook, covered, on Low for 8 to 9 hours or on High for 4 to 4 1/2 hours until rice is tender and liquid is absorbed.

Stir in parsley. Makes about 11 1/2 cups (2.9 L).

1 cup (250 mL): *110 Calories; 0 g Total Fat (0 g Mono, 0 g Poly, 0 g Sat); 0 mg Cholesterol; 24 g Carbohydrate; 4 g Fibre; 5 g Protein; 430 mg Sodium*

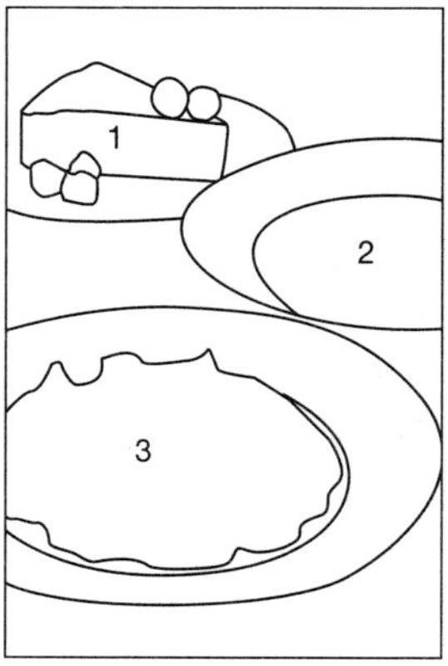

1. Chocolate Tofu Cake, page 147
2. Chipotle Corn Chowder, page 48
3. Walnut Cabbage Bake, page 84

Veggie Meatball Stew

True comfort food. This would be a good meal to let younger kids help make—just make sure to help them cut any larger potatoes.

Baby carrots	**2 cups**	**500 mL**
Baby potatoes, larger ones halved	**1 lb.**	**454 g**
Package of frozen veggie meatballs, thawed	**15 1/2 oz.**	**440 g**
Water	**1 1/2 cups**	**375 mL**
Can of cream of mushroom soup	**10 oz.**	**284 mL**
Pepper	**1/4 tsp.**	**1 mL**
Frozen peas, thawed	**2 cups**	**500 mL**

Layer first 3 ingredients, in order given, in 3 1/2 to 4 quart (3.5 to 4 L) slow cooker.

Combine next 3 ingredients in medium bowl. Pour over meatballs. Do not stir. Cook, covered, on Low for 7 to 8 hours or on High for 3 1/2 to 4 hours.

Add peas. Stir. Cook, covered, on High for 10 minutes. Makes about 7 1/2 cups (1.9 L).

1 cup (250 mL): *220 Calories; 7 g Total Fat (0 g Mono, 0 g Poly, 1 g Sat); trace Cholesterol; 29 g Carbohydrate; 7 g Fibre; 15 g Protein; 720 mg Sodium*

Pictured on page 54.

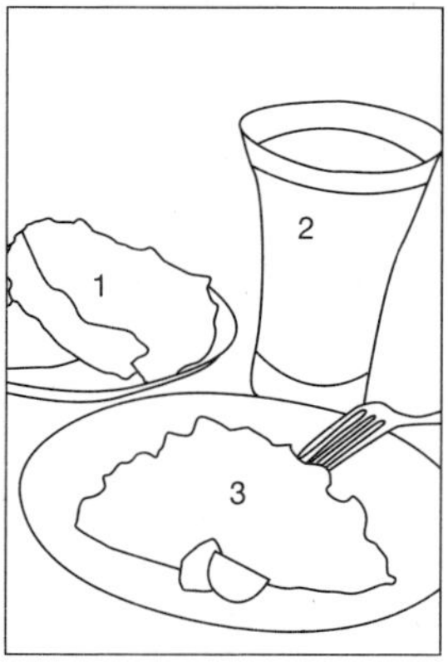

1. Apple Pumpkin Pie Toast, page 26
2. Mango Almond Smoothie, page 24
3. Smoky Mushroom Frittata, page 25

Mushroom Barley Stroganoff

Three types of mushrooms, tender barley and Swiss chard are the stars of this stroganoff stew. Smoky tomato and sour cream notes round out the flavours.

Cooking oil	**1 tbsp.**	**15 mL**
Chopped fresh brown (or white) mushrooms	**3 cups**	**750 mL**
Chopped onion	**2 cups**	**500 mL**
Chopped portobello mushrooms (gills removed, see Tip, page 72)	**2 cups**	**500 mL**
Sliced fresh shiitake mushrooms	**2 cups**	**500 mL**
Salt	**1/2 tsp.**	**2 mL**
Pepper	**1/4 tsp.**	**1 mL**
Garlic cloves, minced (or 1/2 tsp., 2 mL, powder)	**2**	**2**
Dry (or alcohol-free) red wine	**1 cup**	**250 mL**
Chopped Swiss chard (leaves and stems), lightly packed	**4 cups**	**1 L**
Prepared vegetable broth	**3 1/2 cups**	**875 mL**
Can of crushed tomatoes	**14 oz.**	**398 mL**
Pot barley	**1 cup**	**250 mL**
Smoked (sweet) paprika	**1 tsp.**	**5 mL**
Sour cream	**1/2 cup**	**125 mL**
Chopped fresh parsley	**1/4 cup**	**60 mL**
Red wine vinegar	**1 tbsp.**	**15 mL**

Heat cooking oil in large frying pan on medium. Add next 6 ingredients. Cook for about 15 minutes, stirring occasionally, until mushrooms start to brown. Add garlic. Heat and stir for 1 minute.

Add wine. Simmer for 5 minutes. Transfer to greased 3 1/2 to 4 quart (3.5 to 4 L) slow cooker.

Add next 5 ingredients. Stir. Cook, covered, on Low for 6 to 7 hours or on High for 3 to 3 1/2 hours.

Stir in remaining 3 ingredients. Makes about 9 1/2 cups (2.4 L).

__1 cup (250 mL):__ 160 Calories; 1.5 g Total Fat (1 g Mono, 0.5 g Poly, 0 g Sat); 0 mg Cholesterol; 28 g Carbohydrate; 5 g Fibre; 5 g Protein; 430 mg Sodium

Curry Chickpea Rotini

Some say that any cook worth their salt should be able to make a good curry. With this recipe, you can upgrade that to a great curry! Pasta and vegetables are enveloped in a creamy curry sauce studded with sweet bites of apricot.

Rotini pasta	**3 cups**	**750 mL**
Cooking oil	**1 tsp.**	**5 mL**
Can of chickpeas (garbanzo beans), rinsed and drained	**19 oz.**	**540 mL**
Chopped red pepper	**2 cups**	**500 mL**
Chopped celery	**1 cup**	**250 mL**
Chopped onion	**1 cup**	**250 mL**
All-purpose flour	**2 tbsp.**	**30 mL**
Curry powder	**1 tsp.**	**5 mL**
Garlic powder	**1/4 tsp.**	**1 mL**
Ground cumin	**1/4 tsp.**	**1 mL**
Ground ginger	**1/4 tsp.**	**1 mL**
Salt	**1/2 tsp.**	**2 mL**
Pepper	**1/4 tsp.**	**1 mL**
Prepared vegetable broth	**1 cup**	**250 mL**
Chopped dried apricot	**1 cup**	**250 mL**
Evaporated milk (or half-and-half cream)	**1 cup**	**250 mL**

Cook pasta according to package directions. Drain. Return to same pot. Cover to keep warm.

Heat cooking oil in large frying pan on medium. Add next 4 ingredients. Cook for about 10 minutes, stirring often, until onion is softened.

Add next 7 ingredients. Heat and stir for 1 minute.

Slowly add broth, stirring constantly until smooth. Heat and stir until boiling and thickened. Add apricot and evaporated milk. Boil gently for 2 minutes, stirring occasionally. Add to pasta. Stir until coated. Makes about 8 cups (2 L).

1 cup (250 mL): *310 Calories; 3.0 g Total Fat (0 g Mono, 0 g Poly, 0.5 g Sat); 0 mg Cholesterol; 61 g Carbohydrate; 7 g Fibre; 13 g Protein; 400 mg Sodium*

Sweet Chili Veggie Balls

These veggie balls are packed with protein-rich quinoa and vegetables and coated with a spicy sweet and sour sauce. Serve with basmati rice.

Cooking oil	**1/2 tsp.**	**2 mL**
Finely chopped onion	**1/2 cup**	**125 mL**
Finely chopped celery	**1/2 cup**	**125 mL**
Garlic cloves, minced	**2**	**2**
Prepared vegetable broth	**3/4 cup**	**175 mL**
Grated carrot	**1/2 cup**	**125 mL**
Salt	**1/2 tsp.**	**2 mL**
Pepper	**1/4 tsp.**	**1 mL**
Quinoa, rinsed and drained	**1/2 cup**	**125 mL**
Large egg, fork-beaten	**1**	**1**
Quick-cooking rolled oats	**1 cup**	**250 mL**
Cooking oil	**2 tsp.**	**10 mL**
Prepared vegetable broth	**1 1/2 cups**	**375 mL**
Sweet chili sauce	**1/2 cup**	**125 mL**
Cornstarch	**1 tbsp.**	**15 mL**
Lime juice	**1 tbsp.**	**15 mL**

Heat first amount of cooking oil in medium saucepan on medium. Add next 3 ingredients. Cook for about 5 minutes, stirring often, until celery is softened.

Add next 4 ingredients. Stir. Bring to a boil. Add quinoa. Stir. Reduce heat to medium-low. Cook, covered, for about 20 minutes, without stirring, until quinoa is tender and liquid is absorbed. Transfer to large bowl. Let stand for 15 minutes.

Add egg and rolled oats. Mix well. Roll into 1 inch (2.5 cm) balls.

Heat second amount of cooking oil in large frying pan on medium. Add veggie balls. Cook for about 10 minutes, stirring occasionally, until browned.

Whisk remaining 4 ingredients in small bowl. Add to veggie balls. Bring to a boil, stirring occasionally, until sauce is thickened. Serves 6.

1 serving: *200 Calories; 4.5 g Total Fat (2 g Mono, 1 g Poly, 0.5 Sat); 25 mg Cholesterol; 35 g Carbohydrate; 3 g Fibre; 5 g Protein; 580 mg Sodium*

Not Baba's Perogies

These perogies are a lot simpler to make than you may think! Tender sour cream and egg dough holds a rich cottage cheese filling. Resting the rolled-out dough before cutting prevents the circles from shrinking up.

SOUR CREAM DOUGH		
Large egg	**1**	**1**
Sour cream	**1/2 cup**	**125 mL**
Olive oil	**2 tbsp.**	**30 mL**
Salt	**1 tsp.**	**5 mL**
All-purpose flour	**1 3/4 cups**	**425 mL**
FILLING		
Dry curd cottage cheese	**1 1/2 cups**	**375 mL**
Large egg, fork-beaten	**1**	**1**
Salt	**1/4 tsp.**	**1 mL**
Pepper	**1/8 tsp.**	**0.5 mL**

Sour Cream Dough: Beat first 4 ingredients in large bowl until smooth. Slowly add flour, stirring until dough starts to come together. Turn out onto lightly floured surface. Knead for about 3 minutes until ball forms. Wrap with plastic wrap. Let stand for 15 minutes. Divide dough in half. Roll out one dough portion on lightly floured surface to 1/8 inch (3 mm) thickness. Keep remaining half covered with plastic wrap. Loosen and lift dough and sprinkle flour on work surface to prevent sticking. Let stand for 5 minutes. Cut into 3 inch (7.5 cm) circles with biscuit cutter. Roll out scraps to cut more circles. Repeat with remaining dough.

Filling: Combine all 4 ingredients in medium bowl. Place about 1 1/2 tsp. (7 mL) filling in centre of each circle. Fold dough over filling. Press edges together to seal (see Note).

Cook perogies, in batches, in boiling, salted water for about 2 minutes, stirring occasionally, until perogies float to top. Cook for another 3 minutes, stirring occasionally, before removing with slotted spoon to sieve. Drain. Transfer to serving bowl. Makes about 30 perogies. Serves 6.

1 serving: *220 Calories; 5 g Total Fat (2 g Mono, 0.5 g Poly, 2.5 g Sat); 55 mg Cholesterol; 29 g Carbohydrate; trace Fibre; 12 g Protein; 520 mg Sodium*

Note: To store, freeze perogies in a single layer on ungreased baking sheet. Store perogies in a resealable freezer bag for up to 3 months. For best results, cook from frozen.

Biriyani

Chickpeas, creamy paneer cheese and crunchy almonds give this fragrant rice dish substantial main-dish appeal. Paneer is a fresh cheese available in the freezer or deli cheese section of many grocery stores and in specialty Indian food stores. To make this recipe vegan, simply omit the paneer.

Cooking oil	**1 tbsp.**	**15 mL**
Chopped onion	**1 cup**	**250 mL**
Garlic cloves, minced	**2**	**2**
Curry paste	**1 tbsp.**	**15 mL**
Dried crushed chilies	**1/4 tsp.**	**1 mL**
Can of chickpeas (garbanzo beans), rinsed and drained	**19 oz.**	**540 mL**
Brown basmati rice	**1 1/2 cups**	**375 mL**
Diced paneer cheese (about 1/2 inch, 12 mm, pieces)	**1 cup**	**250 mL**
Can of diced tomatoes (with juice)	**28 oz.**	**796 mL**
Prepared vegetable broth (or water)	**1 1/2 cups**	**375 mL**
Saffron threads (optional)	**1/2 tsp.**	**2 mL**
Cinnamon stick (4 inches, 10 cm)	**1**	**1**
Frozen peas, thawed	**1 cup**	**250 mL**
Sliced natural almonds, toasted (see Tip, page 148)	**1/2 cup**	**125 mL**
Chopped fresh cilantro	**2 tbsp.**	**30 mL**

Heat cooking oil in a Dutch oven on medium. Add next 4 ingredients. Cook for about 10 minutes, stirring occasionally, until onion is browned.

Add next 3 ingredients. Heat and stir for 1 minute. Add next 4 ingredients. Stir. Bring to a boil. Reduce heat to medium-low. Cook, covered, for about 1 hour, without lifting lid, until rice is tender.

Stir in peas. Remove from heat. Let stand, covered, for about 5 minutes until peas are heated through. Transfer to serving dish.

Sprinkle with almonds and cilantro. Makes about 8 cups (2 L).

1 cup (250 mL): *370 Calories; 13 g Total Fat (3 g Mono, 1 g Poly, 4.5 g Sat); 20 mg Cholesterol; 51 g Carbohydrate; 8 g Fibre; 16 g Protein; 630 mg Sodium*

Pictured on page 89.

Ginger Tofu Stir-Fry

Don't be put off by the number of ingredients—you can have this dinner on the table in half an hour. The ginger sauce coating every morsel means that it will disappear just as quickly. To make this recipe vegan, use maple or agave syrup instead of honey.

Liquid honey	**2 tbsp.**	**30 mL**
Soy sauce	**2 tbsp.**	**30 mL**
Water	**2 tbsp.**	**30 mL**
Finely grated ginger root	**1 tbsp.**	**15 mL**
Cornstarch	**2 tsp.**	**10 mL**
Garlic cloves, minced	**2**	**2**
Dried crushed chilies	**1/4 tsp.**	**1 mL**
Cooking oil	**2 tsp.**	**10 mL**
Package of firm tofu, drained and cut into 3/4 inch (2 cm) cubes	**12.75 oz.**	**350 g**
Cooking oil	**1 tsp.**	**5 mL**
Broccoli florets	**2 cups**	**500 mL**
Can of cut baby corn, drained	**14 oz.**	**398 mL**
Thinly sliced carrot	**1 cup**	**250 mL**
Sliced red pepper	**1 cup**	**250 mL**
Water	**1/4 cup**	**60 mL**
Roasted sesame seeds	**1 tbsp.**	**15 mL**

Stir first 7 ingredients in small bowl.

Heat large frying pan or wok on medium-high until very hot. Add cooking oil and tofu. Stir-fry for about 5 minutes until starting to brown. Transfer to plate. Cover to keep warm.

Add second amount of cooking oil to frying pan. Add next 4 ingredients. Stir-fry for 2 minutes. Add water. Stir-fry for about 2 minutes until vegetables are tender-crisp. Stir cornstarch mixture. Add to vegetables. Stir-fry for about 2 minutes until boiling and thickened. Add tofu. Stir. Cook for about 1 minute until heated through. Sprinkle with sesame seeds. Makes about 5 cups (1.25 L).

3/4 cup (175 mL): *160 Calories; 6 g Total Fat (1 g Mono, 1 g Poly, 1 g Sat); 0 mg Cholesterol; 17 g Carbohydrate; 3 g Fibre; 11 g Protein; 490 mg Sodium*

Pictured on page 72.

Green Bean Green Curry

To ensure that your curry is vegan, check the list of ingredients on your Thai curry paste—some contain fish sauce. Add more curry paste for a hotter curry.

Can of coconut milk	**14 oz.**	**398 mL**
Prepared vegetable broth	**2/3 cup**	**150 mL**
Soy sauce	**2 tbsp.**	**30 mL**
Brown sugar, packed	**1 tbsp.**	**15 mL**
Thai green curry paste	**1 tbsp.**	**15 mL**
Cooking oil	**1 tbsp.**	**15 mL**
Fresh whole green beans, halved	**3 cups**	**750 mL**
Cauliflower florets	**2 cups**	**500 mL**
Thinly sliced carrot	**1 cup**	**250 mL**
Sliced zucchini (with peel)	**1 1/2 cups**	**375 mL**
Sliced red pepper	**1 cup**	**250 mL**
Cornstarch	**2 tbsp.**	**30 mL**
Lime juice	**2 tbsp.**	**30 mL**
Prepared vegetable broth	**1 tbsp.**	**15 mL**
Chopped fresh basil	**1 tbsp.**	**15 mL**

Whisk first 5 ingredients in medium bowl.

Heat oil in large frying pan on medium-high. Add next 3 ingredients. Cook for about 5 minutes, stirring often, until beans are tender-crisp. Add zucchini, red pepper and coconut milk mixture. Bring to a boil. Reduce heat to medium. Cook for about 8 minutes, stirring occasionally, until beans are tender.

Stir next 3 ingredients in small bowl until smooth. Add to frying pan. Cook and stir for about 2 minutes until boiling and thickened.

Sprinkle with basil. Makes about 6 cups (1.5 L).

1 cup (250 mL): *230 Calories; 17 g Total Fat (2 g Mono, 1 g Poly, 13 g Sat); 0 mg Cholesterol; 18 g Carbohydrate; 4 g Fibre; 5 g Protein; 520 mg Sodium*

Pictured on page 89.

Crusted Tofu with Miso Vegetables

A light, contemporary meal. Marinated tofu is coated and fried, accompanied by miso-sauced bok choy, shiitake mushrooms and green onions.

Prepared vegetable broth	**1 1/3 cups**	**325 mL**
Light miso (fermented soybean paste)	**2 tbsp.**	**30 mL**
Soy sauce	**1 tbsp.**	**15 mL**
Chili paste (sambal oelek)	**1/2 tsp.**	**2 mL**
Garlic clove, minced	**1**	**1**
Package of firm tofu, drained	**12.75 oz.**	**350 g**
Cornstarch	**2 tbsp.**	**30 mL**
Crisp rice cereal, crushed	**1 cup**	**250 mL**
Sesame seeds	**2 tbsp.**	**30 mL**
Cooking oil	**1 tbsp.**	**15 mL**
Whole baby bok choy, quartered	**8**	**8**
Sliced fresh shiitake mushrooms	**2 cups**	**500 mL**
Green onions, cut into 2 inch (5 cm) pieces	**2**	**2**

Whisk first 5 ingredients in small bowl.

Slice tofu in half horizontally into two rectangles. Slice each half diagonally to form a total of 4 triangles. Place tofu in medium resealable freezer bag. Pour broth mixture over top. Seal bag. Turn until coated. Marinate in refrigerator for 6 hours or overnight, turning occasionally. Drain, reserving broth mixture in small bowl. Add cornstarch to broth mixture. Stir until smooth.

Combine cereal and sesame seeds in shallow dish. Press both sides of tofu into cereal mixture until coated. Discard remaining cereal mixture.

Heat cooking oil in large frying pan on medium. Add tofu. Cook for about 5 minutes per side until golden. Transfer to large plate. Cover to keep warm.

Add remaining 3 ingredients to same frying pan. Cook for about 10 minutes, stirring occasionally, until starting to brown. Stir reserved cornstarch mixture. Add to vegetables. Bring to a boil. Heat and stir until boiling and thickened. Divide vegetable mixture onto 4 individual plates. Top with tofu. Serves 4.

***1 serving:** 250 Calories; 11 g Total Fat (3 g Mono, 2 g Poly, 2 g Sat); 0 mg Cholesterol; 24 g Carbohydrate; 5 g Fibre; 17 g Protein; 930 mg Sodium*

Mediterranean Pasta

A pretty pasta dish that's worthy of serving to guests. Use pre-washed spinach to make preparation even easier. You could use Myzithra cheese in place of Parmesan for a more authentic Greek flavour.

Linguine, broken in half	**10 oz.**	**285 g**
Olive oil	**1 tbsp.**	**15 mL**
Sliced red onion	**2/3 cup**	**150 mL**
Garlic cloves, minced (or 1/2 tsp., 2 mL, powder)	**2**	**2**
Chopped fresh spinach leaves, lightly packed	**3 cups**	**750 mL**
Chopped seeded Roma (plum) tomato	**1 1/2 cups**	**375 mL**
Jar of marinated artichokes hearts, drained and halved	**6 oz.**	**170 mL**
Sliced kalamata olives	**1/3 cup**	**75 mL**
Sun-dried tomato pesto	**2 tbsp.**	**30 mL**
Grated Parmesan cheese	**1/4 cup**	**60 mL**
Pine nuts, toasted	**1/4 cup**	**60 mL**
Chopped fresh basil	**1 tbsp.**	**15 mL**
Chopped fresh oregano	**1 tbsp.**	**15 mL**

Cook pasta according to package directions. Drain. Return to same pot. Cover to keep warm.

Heat olive oil in large frying pan on medium. Add onion and garlic. Cook for about 5 minutes, stirring often, until onion is softened.

Add next 5 ingredients. Stir. Cook, covered, for about 2 minutes, stirring once, until spinach is wilted.

Add remaining 4 ingredients and pasta. Toss. Makes about 6 cups (1.5 L).

1 cup (250 mL): *190 Calories; 15 g Total Fat (4.5 g Mono, 2.5 g Poly, 2 g Sat); trace Cholesterol; 25 g Carbohydrate; 3 g Fibre; 10 g Protein; 330 mg Sodium*

Vegan Pad Thai

To make this an easy weeknight meal, marinate the tofu overnight and prep the remaining ingredients while the noodles are soaking.

Finely chopped green onion	2 tbsp.	30 mL
Lemon grass paste	1 tbsp.	15 mL
Garlic cloves, minced	2	2
Chili paste (sambal oelek)	1/4 tsp.	1 mL
Salt	1/4 tsp.	1 mL
Firm tofu, cut into 1/2 inch (12 mm) cubes	12.75 oz.	350 g
Medium rice stick noodles	1/2 lb.	225 g
Sesame (or cooking) oil	1 tbsp.	15 mL
Cooking oil	2 tbsp.	30 mL
Apricot jam	1/4 cup	60 mL
Lime juice	1/4 cup	60 mL
Soy sauce	3 tbsp.	45 mL
Cornstarch	1 tbsp.	15 mL
Chili paste (sambal oelek)	1/2 tsp.	2 mL
Pepper	1/2 tsp.	2 mL
Fresh bean sprouts	2 cups	500 mL
Sliced green onion	1/4 cup	60 mL
Unsalted peanuts, coarsely chopped	1/4 cup	60 mL
Chopped fresh cilantro (or parsley)	2 tbsp.	30 mL

Combine first 5 ingredients in medium bowl. Add tofu. Stir to coat. Cover and refrigerate for at least 2 hours, stirring occasionally. Cover noodles with hot water in medium bowl for about 30 minutes until soft. Drain. Return to same bowl. Drizzle with sesame oil. Toss.

Heat large frying pan or wok on medium-high until very hot. Add oil. Add tofu mixture. Stir-fry for 2 minutes until browned. Transfer to plate. Cover.

Stir next 6 ingredients in small bowl until smooth. Add to same frying pan. Heat and stir until boiling and thickened. Add sprouts, green onion and noodles. Toss until coated. Transfer to large serving dish. Sprinkle with peanuts, cilantro and tofu. Makes about 6 cups (1.5 L).

__1 cup (250 mL):__ 370 Calories; 15 g Total Fat (5 g Mono, 3 g Poly, 2.5 g Sat); 0 mg Cholesterol; 48 g Carbohydrate; 2 g Fibre; 13 g Protein; 660 mg Sodium

Hazelnut Squash Penne

Hazelnuts and sweet butternut squash in a tangy cream sauce accented with aromatic sage.

Whole-wheat penne pasta	**2 cups**	**500 mL**
Butter	**1 tbsp.**	**15 mL**
Olive oil	**1 tbsp.**	**15 mL**
Cauliflower florets (1/2 inch, 12 mm, pieces)	**2 cups**	**500 mL**
Cubed butternut squash (1/2 inch, 12 mm, pieces)	**2 cups**	**500 mL**
Chopped onion	**1 cup**	**250 mL**
All-purpose flour	**1/4 cup**	**60 mL**
Salt	**1/2 tsp.**	**2 mL**
Pepper	**1/4 tsp.**	**1 mL**
Milk	**2 cups**	**500 mL**
Soft goat (chèvre) cheese	**3 1/2 oz.**	**100 g**
Chopped fresh sage	**2 tsp.**	**10 mL**
Coarsely chopped hazelnuts (filberts), toasted (see Tip, page 148)	**1/2 cup**	**125 mL**
Chopped fresh parsley (optional)	**2 tbsp.**	**30 mL**

Cook pasta according to package directions. Drain. Return to same pot. Cover to keep warm.

Heat butter and olive oil in large frying pan on medium-high. Add next 3 ingredients. Cook for about 10 minutes, stirring occasionally, until vegetables are tender-crisp. Reduce heat to medium.

Sprinkle with next 3 ingredients. Heat and stir for 2 minutes.

Slowly add milk, stirring constantly until smooth. Heat and stir until boiling and thickened. Add cheese and sage. Stir until smooth. Add pasta. Stir until coated.

Sprinkle with hazelnuts and parsley. Makes about 7 1/2 cups (1.9 L).

***1 cup (250 mL):** 300 Calories; 13 g Total Fat (6 g Mono, 1 g Poly, 4 g Sat); 15 mg Cholesterol; 36 g Carbohydrate; 5 g Fibre; 12 g Protein; 270 mg Sodium*

Pictured on page 18.

Te Quiero Tacos

You show your family you love them by making great healthy meals—they're going to love these tacos loaded with black beans and all their favourite toppings.

Cooking oil	**1 tsp.**	**5 mL**
Chopped onion	**1/2 cup**	**125 mL**
Grated carrot	**1/2 cup**	**125 mL**
Taco seasoning mix, stir before measuring	**3 tbsp.**	**45 mL**
Canned black beans, rinsed and drained, coarsely mashed	**1 cup**	**250 mL**
Frozen kernel corn, thawed	**1 cup**	**250 mL**
Water	**1/4 cup**	**60 mL**
Hard taco shells	**8**	**8**
Shredded romaine lettuce, lightly packed	**1 cup**	**250 mL**
Diced tomato	**1/2 cup**	**125 mL**
Grated Mexican cheese blend	**1/2 cup**	**125 mL**

Heat cooking oil in large frying pan on medium. Add next 3 ingredients. Cook for about 5 minutes, stirring occasionally, until onion is softened.

Add next 3 ingredients. Cook for about 5 minutes, stirring occasionally, until mixture is heated through.

Arrange taco shells on ungreased baking sheet. Bake in 400°F (200°C) oven for about 5 minutes until warm.

Put lettuce in shells. Spoon bean mixture over lettuce. Sprinkle tomato and cheese over top. Makes 8 tacos.

1 taco: *150 Calories; 4.5 g Total Fat (0 g Mono, 0 g Poly, 2 g Sat); 5 mg Cholesterol; 21 g Carbohydrate; 3 g Fibre; 5 g Protein; 340 mg Sodium*

Quinoa Lentil Pilaf

VEGAN

A pleasant mix of lentils and quinoa with yellow pepper, spinach, fresh herbs and a hint of coriander.

Cooking oil	2 tsp.	10 mL
Sliced fresh white mushrooms	2 cups	500 mL
Chopped onion	1 cup	250 mL
Garlic clove, minced	1	1
Prepared vegetable broth	1 2/3 cups	400 mL
Can of lentils, rinsed and drained	19 oz.	540 mL
Chopped yellow pepper	1 cup	250 mL
Ground coriander	1/2 tsp.	2 mL
Dried crushed chilies	1/4 tsp.	1 mL
Salt	1/8 tsp.	0.5 mL
Pepper	1/2 tsp.	2 mL
Quinoa, rinsed and drained	1 cup	250 mL
Chopped fresh spinach leaves, lightly packed	1 1/2 cups	375 mL
Chopped unsalted, roasted cashews	1/4 cup	60 mL
Chopped fresh mint (or 3/4 tsp., 4 mL, dried)	1 tbsp.	15 mL
Chopped fresh parsley (or 3/4 tsp., 4 mL, flakes)	1 tbsp.	15 mL
Lemon juice	1 tbsp.	15 mL

Heat cooking oil in large saucepan on medium. Add mushrooms and onion. Cook, uncovered, for about 8 minutes, stirring often, until onion is softened.

Add garlic. Heat and stir for about 1 minute until fragrant. Add next 7 ingredients. Stir. Bring to a boil.

Add quinoa. Stir. Reduce heat to medium-low. Simmer, covered, for about 20 minutes, without stirring, until quinoa is tender and liquid is absorbed. Fluff with fork.

Add remaining 5 ingredients. Stir. Makes about 6 cups (1.5 L).

1 cup (250 mL): *280 Calories; 7 g Total Fat (1 g Mono, 0 g Poly, 1 g Sat); 0 mg Cholesterol; 43 g Carbohydrate; 7 g Fibre; 12 g Protein; 360 mg Sodium*

Potato Corn Cakes with Gravy

Keep these nicely browned mashed potato cakes warm in the oven while you make the gravy.

Chopped peeled potato	4 cups	1 L
Large egg, fork-beaten	1	1
Frozen kernel corn, thawed	1 cup	250 mL
2% cottage cheese	1/2 cup	125 mL
Fine dry bread crumbs	1/4 cup	60 mL
Finely chopped red pepper	1/4 cup	60 mL
Thinly sliced green onion	1/4 cup	60 mL
Salt	1/4 tsp.	1 mL
Cayenne pepper	1/8 tsp.	0.5 mL
Cooking oil	3 tbsp.	45 mL
MUSHROOM GRAVY		
Butter (or hard margarine)	2 tbsp.	30 mL
Sliced fresh brown (or white) mushrooms	1 1/2 cups	375 mL
All-purpose flour	3 tbsp.	45 mL
Pepper	1/4 tsp.	1 mL
Prepared vegetable broth	2 cups	500 mL
Dijon mustard	2 tsp.	10 mL

Pour water into large saucepan until about 1 inch (2.5 cm) deep. Add potato. Cover. Bring to a boil. Reduce heat to medium. Boil gently for 12 to 15 minutes until tender. Drain. Mash. Transfer to large bowl. Let stand until cool.

Add next 8 ingredients. Mix well. Using 1/2 cup (125 mL) for each, shape into eight 3 inch (7.5 cm) patties.

Heat cooking oil in large frying pan on medium-high. Cook patties, in 2 batches, for about 3 minutes per side until browned. Transfer to plate. Cover to keep warm. Makes 8 cakes. Wipe frying pan with paper towel.

Mushroom Gravy: Melt butter in same frying pan on medium. Add mushrooms. Cook for about 8 minutes, stirring often, until liquid from mushrooms has been released. Add flour and pepper. Heat and stir for 1 minute. Slowly add broth and mustard, stirring constantly until boiling and thickened. Makes about 2 cups (500 mL) gravy. Spoon over cakes. Serves 4.

1 serving: *380 Calories; 18 g Total Fat (8 g Mono, 3.5 g Poly, 5 g Sat); 50 mg Cholesterol; 44 g Carbohydrate; 4 g Fibre; 11 g Protein; 690 mg Sodium*

Corny Sloppy Joes

A few simple ingredients combine to make a thoroughly likeable family supper. Serve with cut-up veggies. Use vegan buns to make this recipe vegan.

Cooking oil	**1 tsp.**	**5 mL**
Diced onion	**1 cup**	**250 mL**
Finely chopped carrot	**1 cup**	**250 mL**
Package of veggie ground round (see Note)	**12 oz.**	**340 g**
Frozen kernel corn, thawed	**1 cup**	**250 mL**
Can of tomato sauce	**7 1/2 oz.**	**213 mL**
Ketchup	**1/3 cup**	**75 mL**
Whole-wheat (or white) hamburger buns, split and toasted	**4**	**4**

Heat cooking oil in large frying pan on medium. Add onion and carrot. Cook for about 5 minutes, stirring often, until onion is softened.

Add next 4 ingredients. Stir. Cook, covered, on medium-low for about 10 minutes until heated through.

Serve in buns. Makes 4 sloppy joes.

1 sloppy joe: *350 Calories; 3.5 g Total Fat (1 g Mono, 0 g Poly, 0.5 g Sat); 0 mg Cholesterol; 58 g Carbohydrate; 9 g Fibre; 24 g Protein; 1410 mg Sodium*

Note: Veggie ground round is available in the produce section of your grocery store.

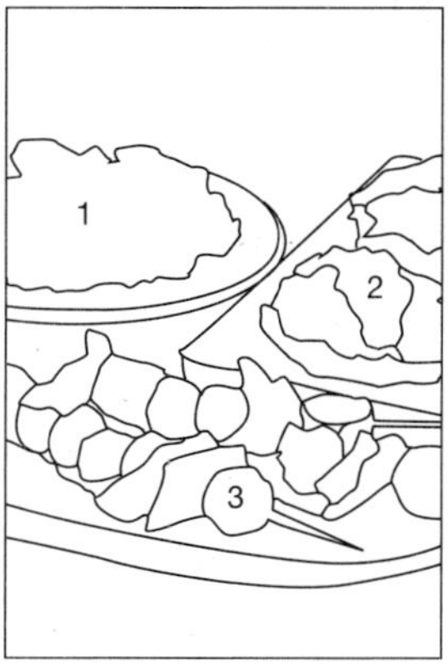

1. Summer Mixed Grill, page 75
2. Grilled Stuffed Mushrooms, page 73
3. Vegetable Polenta Skewers, page 66

Straw and Hay

A Company's Coming Classic. The coloured fettuccine in this creamy, cheesy dish matches the colours of straw and hay.

Fettuccine	**8 oz.**	**225 g**
Spinach fettuccine	**8 oz.**	**225 g**
Butter (or hard margarine)	**2 tbsp.**	**30 mL**
Sliced fresh white mushrooms	**2 cups**	**500 mL**
Can of skim evaporated milk	**13 1/2 oz.**	**385 mL**
Frozen peas, thawed	**2 cups**	**500 mL**
Veggie ham slices, cut in short strips	**5 1/4 oz.**	**155 g**
Grated Parmesan cheese	**1/4 cup**	**60 mL**
Garlic powder	**1/4 tsp.**	**1 mL**
Salt	**1/2 tsp.**	**2 mL**
Pepper	**1/4 tsp.**	**1 mL**
Grated Parmesan cheese	**1/4 cup**	**60 mL**

Cook both pastas according to package directions. Drain. Return to same pot. Cover to keep warm.

Melt butter in large frying pan on medium. Add mushrooms. Cook for about 10 minutes, stirring occasionally, until browned.

Stir in milk and peas. Simmer, covered, for about 2 minutes until peas are tender. Add to pasta.

Add next 5 ingredients. Toss. Transfer to plate.

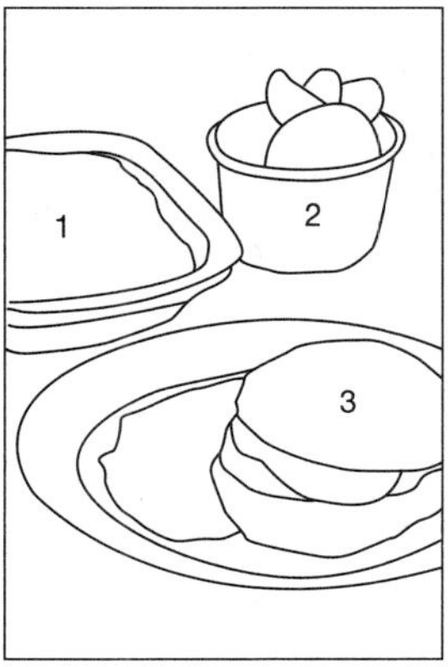

Sprinkle with second amount of cheese. Makes about 12 cups (3 L).

***1 cup (250 mL):** 180 Calories; 4.5 g Total Fat (1 g Mono, 0 g Poly, 2 g Sat); 10 mg Cholesterol; 30 g Carbohydrate; 2 g Fibre; 14 g Protein; 360 mg Sodium*

1. Whisky Baked Beans, page 139
2. Chocolate Banana Almond Ice Cream, page 151
3. Smoky Black Bean Burgers, page 60

Butternut Pesto Risotto

The butternut squash breaks down a bit as the risotto cooks, lending this dish a lovely golden colour. Extra punches are provided by red pepper, parsley and pine nuts. For a finishing touch, garnish with a bit of fresh basil and a sprinkle of extra Parmesan cheese.

Prepared vegetable broth	**4 cups**	**1 L**
Olive oil	**1 tsp.**	**5 mL**
Chopped celery	**1 cup**	**250 mL**
Chopped onion	**1 cup**	**250 mL**
Pepper	**1/4 tsp.**	**1 mL**
Garlic cloves, minced	**2**	**2**
Diced butternut squash (see Tip, page 93)	**2 cups**	**500 mL**
Arborio rice	**1 cup**	**250 mL**
Dry (or alcohol-free) white wine	**1/2 cup**	**125 mL**
Diced red pepper	**1 cup**	**250 mL**
Grated Parmesan cheese	**1/2 cup**	**125 mL**
Basil pesto	**2 tbsp.**	**30 mL**
Pine nuts, toasted (see Tip, page 148)	**2 tbsp.**	**30 mL**
Chopped fresh parsley	**1 tbsp.**	**15 mL**
Lemon juice	**1 tbsp.**	**15 mL**

Bring broth to a boil in small saucepan. Reduce heat to low. Cover to keep warm.

Heat olive oil in large saucepan on medium. Add next 4 ingredients. Cook for about 8 minutes, stirring often, until celery is softened.

Add squash and rice. Heat and stir for 1 minute. Add wine. Heat and stir for about 1 minute until liquid is evaporated. Add 1 cup (250 mL) hot broth, stirring constantly until broth is almost absorbed. Repeat 2 more times, adding broth 1 cup (250 mL) at a time. Add red pepper and remaining cup of broth, stirring constantly until broth is absorbed and rice is tender and creamy.

Stir in remaining 5 ingredients. Makes about 5 2/3 cups (1.4 L).

1 cup (250 mL): *260 Calories; 7 g Total Fat (1.5 g Mono, 1 g Poly, 1.5 g Sat); 5 mg Cholesterol; 41 g Carbohydrate; 3 g Fibre; 7 g Protein; 570 mg Sodium*

Pictured on page 18.

Sweet Potato Ravioli

Ready-to-use wonton wrappers enclose a cheesy sweet potato filling. Cooked ravioli are topped with a lime-accented buttery sauce.

Chopped peeled orange-fleshed sweet potato	**4 cups**	**1 L**
Goat (chèvre) cheese, cut up	**3 oz.**	**85 g**
Smoked (sweet) paprika	**1 tsp.**	**5 mL**
Salt	**1/2 tsp.**	**2 mL**
Pepper	**1/2 tsp.**	**2 mL**
Wonton wrappers (see Note)	**72**	**72**
Butter (or hard margarine)	**1/3 cup**	**75 mL**
Pine nuts	**1/4 cup**	**60 mL**
Chopped fresh cilantro (or parsley)	**1 tbsp.**	**15 mL**
Lime juice	**2 tsp.**	**10 mL**
Grated lime zest (see Tip, page 33)	**1/2 tsp.**	**2 mL**

Pour water into large saucepan until about 1 inch (2.5 cm) deep. Bring to a boil. Reduce heat to medium. Boil gently, covered, for 12 to 15 minutes until sweet potato is tender. Drain. Mash.

Add next 4 ingredients. Mash until combined.

Arrange 36 wrappers on work surface. Place 1 tbsp. (15 mL) sweet potato mixture in centre of each wrapper. Brush water over edges of wrappers. Cover with remaining wrappers. Press edges to seal.

Melt butter in large frying pan on medium. Add pine nuts. Heat and stir for about 1 minute until nuts are browned. Add remaining 3 ingredients. Stir. Remove from heat. Cover to keep warm.

Cook half of ravioli in boiling, salted water for about 5 minutes, stirring occasionally, until wrappers are tender but firm. Transfer with slotted spoon to sieve. Drain. Transfer to butter mixture. Toss gently to coat. Cover to keep warm. Repeat with remaining ravioli. Serves 6.

***1 serving:** 350 Calories; 19 g Total Fat (4.5 g Mono, 2.5 g Poly, 9 g Sat); 60 mg Cholesterol; 37 g Carbohydrate; 4 g Fibre; 10 g Protein; 650 mg Sodium*

Note: Wonton wrappers are often found in the produce section of grocery stores with other fresh noodles or in the Asian section of the freezer department.

Eggplant and Bean Ragout

Browned eggplant slices over a bean ragout with mild goat cheese flavours. Serve with crusty rolls and a leafy salad.

Olive (or cooking) oil	1 tsp.	5 mL
Chopped fennel bulb (white part only)	1 cup	250 mL
Chopped onion	1 cup	250 mL
Can of navy beans, rinsed and drained	19 oz.	540 mL
Prepared vegetable broth	1 1/4 cups	300 mL
Dry (or alcohol-free) white wine	1/2 cup	125 mL
Goat (chèvre) cheese, cut up	2 oz.	57 g
Pepper	1/4 tsp.	1 mL
All-purpose flour	1/4 cup	60 mL
Salt	1 tsp.	5 mL
Pepper	1 tsp.	5 mL
Garlic powder	1/2 tsp.	2 mL
Small eggplants (about 1/2 lb., 225 g, each), cut crosswise into 1/2 inch (12 mm) thick slices	2	2
Olive oil	2 tbsp.	30 mL
Finely chopped fresh basil	1 tbsp.	15 mL
Finely chopped fresh parsley	1 tbsp.	15 mL

Heat first amount of olive oil in large saucepan. Add fennel and onion. Cook for about 8 minutes, stirring often, until fennel is softened. Add next 5 ingredients. Stir. Bring to a boil. Simmer, uncovered, for 5 minutes. Remove half of mixture. Process with hand blender or in blender with on/off motion until almost smooth. Return to pan. Stir. Reduce heat to low. Cover to keep warm.

Combine next 4 ingredients in large shallow dish. Press both sides of eggplant slices into flour mixture until coated. Brush off excess flour mixture. Discard any remaining flour mixture.

Heat 1 tbsp. (15 mL) of second amount of olive oil in large frying pan on medium. Add half of eggplant. Cook for about 6 minutes per side until tender and golden. Transfer to large plate. Cover to keep warm. Repeat with remaining olive oil and eggplant. Spread bean mixture on 4 individual plates. Layer with eggplant. Sprinkle with basil and parsley. Serves 4.

1 serving: *250 Calories; 11 g Total Fat (6 g Mono, 1 g Poly, 3 g Sat); 5 mg Cholesterol; 26 g Carbohydrate; 11 g Fibre; 8 g Protein; 380 mg Sodium*

Hoppin' John

VEGAN

Hoppin' John is a classic Southern dish that contains black-eyed peas, rice and smoked pork hock or ham. Using smoked paprika here adds a touch of smokiness without the meat. Serving this on New Year's Day is supposed to bring good luck!

Water	**2 cups**	**500 mL**
Long-grain brown rice	**1 cup**	**250 mL**
Cooking oil	**1 tsp.**	**5 mL**
Diced celery	**1 cup**	**250 mL**
Diced onion	**1 cup**	**250 mL**
Garlic cloves, minced (or 1/2 tsp., 2 mL, powder)	**2**	**2**
Can of black-eyed peas, rinsed and drained	**19 oz.**	**540 mL**
Tomato juice	**1 cup**	**250 mL**
Diced green pepper	**1 cup**	**250 mL**
Diced red pepper	**1 cup**	**250 mL**
Cajun seasoning	**1 tbsp.**	**15 mL**
Smoked (sweet) paprika	**1 tsp.**	**5 mL**
Dried thyme	**1/2 tsp.**	**2 mL**
Bay leaf	**1**	**1**
Salt	**1/4 tsp.**	**1 mL**
Cayenne pepper	**1/8 tsp.**	**0.5 mL**
Chopped green onion	**2 tbsp.**	**30 mL**

Bring water to a boil in large saucepan. Add rice. Stir. Reduce heat to medium-low. Cook, covered, for about 40 minutes, without lifting lid, until liquid is absorbed and rice is tender. Remove from heat. Let stand, covered, for 5 minutes. Fluff with fork.

Heat cooking oil in large frying pan on medium. Add next 3 ingredients. Cook for about 8 minutes, stirring occasionally, until celery is softened.

Add remaining 10 ingredients. Stir. Reduce heat to medium-low. Cook, covered, for about 10 minutes until green pepper is tender-crisp. Add rice. Stir.

Sprinkle with green onion. Makes about 6 cups (1.5 L).

1 cup (250 mL): *210 Calories; 2.5 g Total Fat (0.5 g Mono, 0.5 g Poly, 0 g Sat); 0 mg Cholesterol; 42 g Carbohydrate; 7 g Fibre; 7 g Protein; 890 mg Sodium*

Vietnamese Omelette

This thin omelette is folded over a filling of richly seasoned stir-fried Asian ingredients. Use a mixture of mushrooms such as shiitake and oyster, if desired.

Large eggs	**8**	**8**
Water	**1/2 cup**	**125 mL**
Salt	**1/4 tsp.**	**1 mL**
Pepper	**1/8 tsp.**	**0.5 mL**
Cooking oil	**1 tsp.**	**5 mL**
Sliced fresh brown (or white) mushrooms	**2 cups**	**500 mL**
Thinly sliced bok choy	**2 cups**	**500 mL**
Sliced red pepper	**1 cup**	**250 mL**
Sliced green pepper	**1/4 cup**	**60 mL**
Grated carrot	**1 cup**	**250 mL**
Garlic cloves, minced (or 1/2 tsp., 2 mL, powder)	**2**	**2**
Finely grated ginger root	**1 tbsp.**	**15 mL**
Soy sauce	**1 tbsp.**	**15 mL**
Rice vinegar	**2 tsp.**	**10 mL**
Dried crushed chilies	**1/2 tsp.**	**2 mL**
Fresh bean sprouts	**1 cup**	**250 mL**

Whisk first 4 ingredients in large bowl. Pour into greased parchment paper–lined 9 x 13 inch (23 x 33 cm) pan. Bake in 400°F (200°C) oven for about 10 minutes until set. Keep warm.

Heat cooking oil in large frying pan on medium-high. Add mushrooms. Cook for about 5 minutes, stirring often, until starting to brown. Add next 5 ingredients. Stir-fry for about 3 minutes until bok choy is tender-crisp.

Add remaining 5 ingredients. Stir-fry for 1 minute until bean sprouts start to soften. Invert omelette onto cutting board. Spoon vegetable mixture lengthwise along one half of omelette. Fold over to cover filling. Cuts into 4 pieces.

1 piece: *170 Calories; 9 g Total Fat (4 g Mono, 1.5 g Poly, 2.5 g Sat); 275 mg Cholesterol; 10 g Carbohydrate; 2 g Fibre; 12 g Protein; 520 mg Sodium*

Tater Cakes

A healthier and more refined cousin of the tater tot. These cakes are a great way to use up whatever leftover veggies you have on hand, and can be served on their own or with ketchup.

Grated peeled potato	**1 1/2 cups**	**375 mL**
Grated yellow turnip (or rutabaga)	**1/2 cup**	**125 mL**
Finely chopped broccoli	**1/3 cup**	**75 mL**
Finely chopped carrot	**1/3 cup**	**75 mL**
Water	**1 tbsp.**	**15 mL**
Large egg	**1**	**1**
All-purpose flour	**2 tbsp.**	**30 mL**
Onion powder	**1/4 tsp.**	**1 mL**
Seasoned salt	**1/4 tsp.**	**1 mL**
Cooking oil	**2 tbsp.**	**30 mL**

Combine first 4 ingredients in medium microwave-safe bowl. Sprinkle with water. Microwave, covered, on high (100%) for about 5 minutes, stirring once, until vegetables are softened (see Tip, below).

Beat next 4 ingredients in small bowl. Add vegetables. Stir well. Divide into 12 portions. Form into 3 inch (7.5 cm) cakes.

Heat 1 tbsp. (15 mL) cooking oil in large frying pan on medium. Cook half of cakes for about 2 minutes per side until browned and crisp. Repeat with remaining cooking oil and cakes. Makes about 12 tater cakes.

1 tater cake: *45 Calories; 2.5 g Total Fat (1.5 g Mono, 0.5 g Poly, 0 g Sat); 10 mg Cholesterol; 5 g Carbohydrate; trace Fibre; 1 g Protein; 45 mg Sodium*

tip The microwaves used in our test kitchen are 900 watts—but microwave are sold in many different powers. You should be able to find the wattage of yours by opening the door and looking for the mandatory label. If your microwave is more than 900 watts, you may need to reduce the cooking time. If it's less than 900 watts, you'll probably need to increase the cooking time.

Balsamic Glazed Beets

Quickly transform simple canned beets into a gourmet side dish!

Butter	**1 tbsp.**	**15 mL**
Cans of rosebud (baby) beets (14 oz., 398 mL, each), drained and quartered	**2**	**2**
Balsamic vinegar	**2 tbsp.**	**30 mL**
Salt, sprinkle		
Pepper, sprinkle		
Soft goat (chèvre) cheese	**2 oz.**	**57 g**
Prepared horseradish	**1 tbsp.**	**15 mL**
Chopped pistachios	**2 tbsp.**	**30 mL**
Chopped fresh chives	**1 tbsp.**	**15 mL**

Melt butter in medium frying pan on medium-high. Add next 4 ingredients. Cook for about 3 minutes, stirring occasionally, until beets are glazed. Transfer to serving bowl.

Combine goat cheese and horseradish in small bowl. Crumble over beets.

Sprinkle with pistachios and chives. Makes about 3 cups (750 mL).

1/2 cup (125 mL): *90 Calories; 5 g Total Fat (1.5 g Mono, 0 g Poly, 2.5 g Sat); 10 mg Cholesterol; 8 g Carbohydrate; 2 g Fibre; 3 g Protein; 220 mg Sodium*

Pictured on page 143.

Zoom Zoom Zucchini

This side dish is ready in a jiffy and makes a nice accompaniment for egg dishes, pasta or rice. A bit like ratatouille on speed dial.

Olive (or cooking) oil	**1 tsp.**	**5 mL**
Chopped onion	**1 cup**	**250 mL**
Chopped zucchini (with peel), about 1 inch (2.5 cm) pieces	**3 cups**	**750 mL**
Chopped red pepper	**1 cup**	**250 mL**
Chopped yellow pepper	**1 cup**	**250 mL**
Jar of marinated artichoke hearts, drained and chopped	**6 oz.**	**170 mL**
Prepared bruschetta topping	**1/2 cup**	**125 mL**

Heat olive oil in large frying pan or wok on medium-high. Add onion. Stir-fry for about 3 minutes until onion is softened.

Add next 4 ingredients. Stir-fry for about 5 minutes until vegetables are tender-crisp.

Add bruschetta. Stir-fry for 1 minute. Makes about 5 cups (1.25 L).

1/2 cup (125 mL): *80 Calories; 4.5 g Total Fat (0 g Mono, 0 g Poly, 1 g Sat); 0 mg Cholesterol; 7 g Carbohydrate; 1 g Fibre; 1 g Protein; 140 mg Sodium*

Pictured on page 143.

Swiss Stuffed Potatoes

Appealing twice-baked potatoes that are stuffed with mashed potato, tomato, yellow pepper and melted Swiss cheese.

Large unpeeled baking potatoes	**4**	**4**
Cooking oil	**1 tsp.**	**5 mL**
Chopped onion	**3/4 cup**	**175 mL**
Garlic clove, minced	**1**	**1**
Granulated sugar	**1 tsp.**	**5 mL**
Dried thyme	**1/4 tsp.**	**1 mL**
Chopped seeded tomato	**1/2 cup**	**125 mL**
Sour cream	**1/2 cup**	**125 mL**
Grated Swiss cheese	**1/3 cup**	**75 mL**
Finely chopped yellow pepper	**1/4 cup**	**60 mL**
Dijon mustard	**1 tsp.**	**5 mL**
Salt	**1/2 tsp.**	**2 mL**
Pepper	**1/4 tsp.**	**1 mL**
Cooking spray		
Grated Swiss cheese	**1/4 cup**	**60 mL**

Wrap each potato in foil. Bake directly on centre rack in 425°F (220°C) oven for about 1 1/2 hours until tender. Transfer to cutting board. Carefully remove foil. Let stand until cool enough to handle. Cut potatoes in half lengthwise. Scoop out pulp, leaving 1/4 inch (6 mm) shell. Mash pulp in large bowl.

Heat cooking oil in medium frying pan on medium. Add next 4 ingredients. Cook for about 5 minutes, stirring often, until onion is softened. Add to mashed potato.

Add next 7 ingredients. Stir.

Spray outside of potato shells with cooking spray. Arrange, cut-side up, on baking sheet. Fill with mashed potato mixture.

Sprinkle with second amount of cheese. Bake in 425°F (220°C) oven for about 25 minutes until heated through and cheese is golden. Makes 8 stuffed potatoes.

***1 stuffed potato:** 220 Calories; 5 g Total Fat (1.5 g Mono, 0 g Poly, 3 g Sat); 15 mg Cholesterol; 37 g Carbohydrate; 3 g Fibre; 7 g Protein; 180 mg Sodium*

Pictured on page 143.

Mushroom Tarragon Stuffing

Did you end up with leftover baguettes? Use them to make this versatile side dish. Alternately, freeze the ends of baguettes (or French bread) that don't get eaten until you have enough for this recipe.

Butter (or hard margarine)	**2 tbsp.**	**30 mL**
Thinly sliced onion	**2 cups**	**500 mL**
Thinly sliced celery	**1/2 cup**	**125 mL**
Sliced fresh brown (or white) mushrooms	**3 cups**	**750 mL**
Garlic clove, minced (or 1/4 tsp., 1 mL, powder)	**1**	**1**
Salt	**1/4 tsp.**	**1 mL**
Pepper	**1/4 tsp.**	**1 mL**
Cubed day-old baguette bread	**8 cups**	**2 L**
Large egg, fork-beaten	**1**	**1**
Prepared vegetable broth	**3/4 cup**	**175 mL**
Half-and-half cream	**1/4 cup**	**60 mL**
Sweet sherry	**1/4 cup**	**60 mL**
Lemon juice	**1 tbsp.**	**15 mL**
Chopped fresh tarragon (or 1/4 tsp., 1 mL, dried)	**1 tsp.**	**5 mL**

Melt butter in large frying pan on medium. Add onion and celery. Cook for about 12 minutes, stirring often, until celery is softened.

Add next 4 ingredients. Cook for about 5 minutes, stirring often, until liquid from mushrooms has evaporated. Transfer to extra-large bowl.

Add bread cubes. Stir.

Combine remaining 6 ingredients in small bowl. Add to bread cube mixture. Stir until moistened. Transfer to greased 2 quart (2 L) casserole.

Bake, covered, in 375°F (190°C) oven for 20 minutes. Bake, uncovered, for another 20 minutes until top is golden. Makes about 7 cups (1.75 L).

1 cup (250 mL): *100 Calories; 4.5 g Total Fat (1.5 g Mono, 0 g Poly, 3 g Sat); 30 mg Cholesterol; 9 g Carbohydrate; trace Fibre; 3 g Protein; 220 mg Sodium*

Curry Roasted Corn

Sweet corn and curry play nicely together. Use vegan butter or cooking oil to make this a vegan side dish.

Butter (or hard margarine), softened	**2 tbsp.**	**30 mL**
Curry powder	**1 tbsp.**	**15 mL**
Brown sugar, packed	**1 tsp.**	**5 mL**
Salt	**1/4 tsp.**	**1 mL**
Pepper	**1/4 tsp.**	**1 mL**
Medium corncobs, cut crosswise into 3 pieces each	**4**	**4**

Combine first 5 ingredients in small cup.

Arrange corn in shallow 2 quart (2 L) casserole. Brush with butter mixture. Cook, covered, in 400°F (200°C) oven for about 30 minutes until corn is tender. Makes 12 pieces.

1 piece: *100 Calories; 3 g Total Fat (1 g Mono, 0.5 g Poly, 1.5 g Sat); 5 mg Cholesterol; 19 g Carbohydrate; 3 g Fibre; 3 g Protein; 75 mg Sodium*

Whisky Baked Beans

A simple and quick version of slow-baked beans, with an interesting addition of whisky in the sauce.

Bourbon whisky	**1/4 cup**	**60 mL**
Hickory barbecue sauce	**1/4 cup**	**60 mL**
Maple syrup	**1/4 cup**	**60 mL**
Apple cider vinegar	**1 tbsp.**	**15 mL**
Dry mustard	**1 tbsp.**	**15 mL**
Salt	**1/4 tsp.**	**1 mL**
Pepper	**1/4 tsp**	**1 mL**
Cans of navy beans (19 oz., 540 mL, each), rinsed and drained	**2**	**2**
Can of diced tomatoes (with juice)	**14 oz.**	**398 mL**
Finely chopped onion	**1 cup**	**250 mL**

Combine first 7 ingredients in large bowl.

Add remaining 3 ingredients. Stir. Transfer to ungreased 2 quart (2 L) casserole. Bake, covered, in 375°F (190°C) oven for 1 hour. Bake, uncovered, for about 10 minutes until sauce is thickened. Makes about 5 cups (1.25 L).

1 cup (250 mL): *200 Calories; 0 g Total Fat (0 g Mono, 0 g Poly, 0 g Sat); 0 mg Cholesterol; 30 g Carbohydrate; 10 g Fibre; 7 g Protein; 760 mg Sodium*

Pictured on page 126.

Chutney Bean Dip

You'll have this five-ingredient dip ready in less than 10 minutes. Use a medium or hot curry paste if you like a little extra heat. Serve with potato chips, pitas, tortilla chips, veggies, apple slices or crackers.

Can of white kidney beans, rinsed and drained	**19 oz.**	**540 mL**
Plain yogurt	**1/3 cup**	**75 mL**
Mango chutney	**1/4 cup**	**60 mL**
Mild curry paste	**1 tsp.**	**5 mL**
Thinly sliced green onion	**2 tsp.**	**10 mL**

Process first 4 ingredients in food processor, scraping down sides if necessary, until smooth. Transfer to serving bowl.

Stir in green onion. Makes about 1 7/8 cups (450 mL).

1/4 cup (60 mL): *80 Calories; 0.5 g Total Fat (0 g Mono, 0 g Poly, 0 g Sat); 0 mg Cholesterol; 15 g Carbohydrate; 5 g Fibre; 4 g Protein; 240 mg Sodium*

Cheese Sauce

Serve this creamy sauce over Stuffed Summer Squash (page 75) or steamed veggies such as cauliflower or broccoli. Or stir in a little salsa and use it as a dip for tortilla or pita chips.

Butter	**2 tbsp.**	**30 mL**
All-purpose flour	**2 tbsp.**	**30 mL**
Milk, warmed	**1 cup**	**250 mL**
White Cheddar cheese	**1/2 cup**	**125 mL**
Gruyère cheese	**1/2 cup**	**125 mL**
Salt	**1/4 tsp.**	**1 mL**
White pepper	**1/4 tsp.**	**1 mL**

Melt butter in medium sauce pan over medium. Whisk in flour and cook for 1 minute, stirring constantly. Gradually whisk in warmed milk, stirring constantly, until thickened, about 7 minutes. Remove from heat and stir in cheeses, salt and pepper, until everything is blended. Makes 1 1/2 cups.

1 serving: *140 Calories; 10 g Total Fat (3 g Mono, 0 g Poly, 6 g Sat); 30 mg Cholesterol; 5 g Carbohydrate; 0 g Fibre; 7 g Protein; 220 mg Sodium*

Sweet and Spicy Edamame

Crisp soybeans that are perfectly coated with zippy Thai spices.

Brown sugar, packed	**2 tbsp.**	**30 mL**
Cooking oil	**2 tbsp.**	**30 mL**
Chili paste (sambal oelek)	**1 tbsp.**	**15 mL**
Ground ginger	**1 tsp.**	**5 mL**
Garlic powder	**1/2 tsp.**	**2 mL**
Salt	**1/2 tsp.**	**2 mL**
Frozen, shelled edamame (soybeans), thawed and blotted dry	**3 cups**	**750 mL**

Stir first 6 ingredients in large bowl until sugar is dissolved.

Add edamame. Toss until coated. Transfer to parchment paper–lined baking sheet. Bake in 300°F (150°C) oven for about 1 1/2 hours, stirring every 30 minutes, until browned and crisp. Makes about 1 2/3 cups (400 mL).

1/3 cup (75 mL): *190 Calories; 9 g Total Fat (3.5 g Mono, 1.5 g Poly, 0 g Sat); 0 mg Cholesterol; 18 g Carbohydrate; 4 g Fibre; 10 g Protein; 310 mg Sodium*

Pictured on page 90.

Super Sesame Bars

A snack that is easy to make and take anywhere. Choose nut-free granola and you can send these to school with your kids without fear of allergies or sensitivities.

Golden corn syrup	**1 cup**	**250 mL**
Brown sugar, packed	**1 cup**	**250 mL**
Tahini (sesame paste)	**1 cup**	**250 mL**
Granola	**3 1/2 cups**	**875 mL**
Roasted sesame seeds	**1/2 cup**	**125 mL**

Combine corn syrup and sugar in large saucepan. Bring to a boil on medium, stirring occasionally. Remove from heat.

Stir tahini into sugar mixture until smooth. Add granola. Stir. Press into parchment paper–lined 9 x 13 inch (23 x 33 cm) pan.

Sprinkle with sesame seeds. Press lightly. Let stand for about 2 hours until cooled and set. Cuts into 48 triangles.

1 triangle: *120 Calories; 4.5 g Total Fat (0 g Mono, 0 g Poly, 0.5 g Sat); 0 mg Cholesterol; 19 g Carbohydrate; 2 g Fibre; 2 g Protein; 25 mg Sodium*

Pictured on page 90.

1. Zoom Zoom Zucchini, page 135
2. Balsamic Glazed Beets, page 134
3. Swiss Stuffed Potatoes, page 136

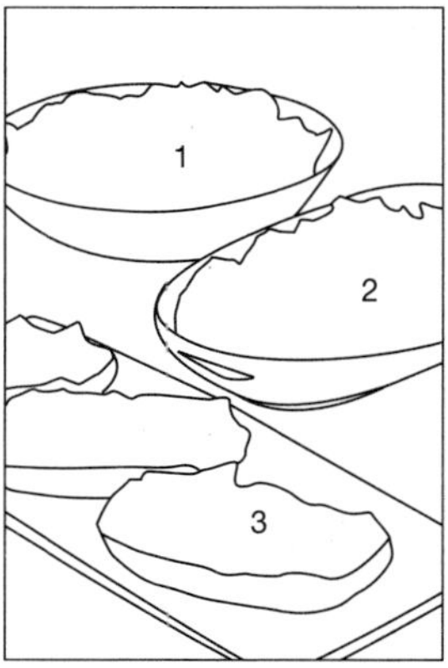

Nutty Candy Bars

A Company's Coming Classic. So good—so rich. Full of cereal, peanut butter and peanuts. To make this vegan, use vegan chocolate chips and a vegan butter substitute.

Corn syrup	**1 cup**	**250 mL**
Granulated sugar	**1/2 cup**	**125 mL**
Smooth peanut butter	**1 cup**	**250 mL**
Vanilla extract	**1 tsp.**	**5 mL**
Cornflakes cereal	**2 cups**	**500 mL**
Crisp rice cereal	**2 cups**	**500 mL**
Salted peanuts	**1 cup**	**250 mL**
TOPPING		
Semi-sweet chocolate chips	**2 cups**	**500 mL**
Butter (hard margarine)	**1/4 cup**	**60 mL**

Heat and stir corn syrup and sugar in large saucepan on medium until sugar is dissolved.

Stir in peanut butter and vanilla.

Add next 3 ingredients. Stir well. Press into greased 9 x 13 (23 x 33 cm) pan. Cool.

Topping: Melt chocolate chips and butter in small saucepan on low, stirring often. Spread over top. Let stand to harden. Cuts into 54 squares.

1 square: *130 Calories; 7 g Total Fat (1 g Mono, 0 g Poly, 2.5 g Sat); trace Cholesterol; 18 g Carbohydrate; 1 g Fibre; 3 g Protein; 95 mg Sodium*

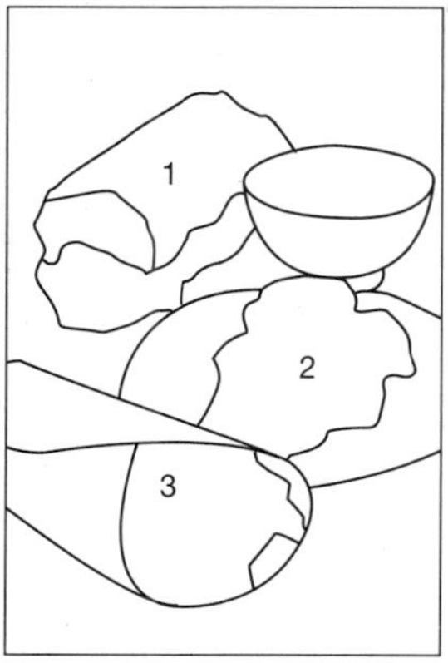

1. Pepper Aioli Baguette, page 63
2. Portobello "Steak" Fajitas, page 67
3. Chili Tofu Wraps, page 61

Power Poppers

These moist cookies not only have the energy to keep you going but also the power to attract many admirers with their chocolatey flavour and bursts of sweet apricot.

Peanut butter	1 1/2 cups	375 mL
Brown sugar, packed	3/4 cup	175 mL
Can of pure pumpkin (no spices) (see Tip, page 26)	14 oz.	398 mL
Vanilla extract	1 tsp.	5 mL
Whole-wheat flour	3 cups	750 mL
Cocoa, sifted if lumpy	1/4 cup	60 mL
Baking powder	2 tsp.	10 mL
Ground cinnamon	1/2 tsp.	2 mL
Salt	1/2 tsp.	2 mL
Dark chocolate chips	2 cups	500 mL
Chopped dried apricots	1 cup	250 mL

Beat peanut butter and sugar in large bowl until light and creamy.

Add pumpkin and vanilla. Beat until smooth.

Combine next 5 ingredients in medium bowl. Add to peanut butter mixture in 2 additions, mixing well after each addition, until no dry flour remains.

Add chocolate chips and apricots. Mix well. Drop, using 1 tbsp. (15 mL) for each, onto greased cookie sheets. Flatten slightly with fork. Bake in 350°F (175°C) oven for about 10 minutes until bottom is lightly browned. Let stand on cookie sheets for 5 minutes before removing to wire racks to cool. Makes about 84 poppers.

1 popper: *100 Calories; 4.5 g Total Fat (0 g Mono, 0 g Poly, 1.5 g Sat); 0 mg Cholesterol; 14 g Carbohydrate; 2 g Fibre; 3 g Protein; 50 mg Sodium*

Chocolate Tofu Cake

A decadent, silky chocolate mousse that is a real delight. If you can't find seedless raspberry jam, press seeded jam through a fine strainer and discard the seeds.

Graham cracker crumbs	1 1/4 cups	300 mL
Cooking oil	1/4 cup	60 mL
Brown sugar, packed	2 tbsp.	30 mL
Hot strong prepared coffee	3/4 cup	175 mL
Cocoa, sifted if lumpy	1/2 cup	125 mL
Box of unsweetened chocolate baking squares, chopped	8 oz.	225 g
Seedless raspberry jam (not jelly)	1/2 cup	125 mL
Packages of firm silken tofu (12.3 oz., 349 g, each)	2	2
Granulated sugar	1 cup	250 mL
Vanilla extract	1 tsp.	5 mL
Salt	1/8 tsp.	0.5 mL
Fresh (or frozen, thawed) raspberries	24	24

Combine first 3 ingredients in medium bowl. Press firmly into bottom of greased 9 inch (23 cm) springform pan. Bake in 350°F (175°C) oven for 10 minutes. Let stand until cool.

Heat and stir coffee and cocoa in small saucepan on medium-low until cocoa is dissolved. Add chocolate and jam. Stir until smooth.

Process next 4 ingredients in food processor until smooth. Add chocolate mixture. Process, scraping down sides if necessary, until smooth. Spread over crust. Chill overnight until set.

Arrange raspberries on centre of cake. Cuts into 12 wedges.

1 wedge: *330 Calories; 18 g Total Fat (3 g Mono, 1 g Poly, 7 g Sat); 0 mg Cholesterol; 46 g Carbohydrate; 5 g Fibre; 7 g Protein; 125 mg Sodium*

Pictured on page 107.

Almond Fruit Bars

VEGAN

No-bake bars packed with an appetizing medley of fruit, almonds and seeds. Perfect to bring hiking or camping. You can wrap bars individually in plastic wrap and store in an airtight container in the fridge for up to two months.

Slivered almonds, toasted (see Tip, below)	**2 cups**	**500 mL**
Chopped pitted dates	**2 cups**	**500 mL**
Chopped dried apricots	**1 cup**	**250 mL**
Almond butter	**1/4 cup**	**60 mL**
Lemon juice	**1 tbsp.**	**15 mL**
Grated lemon zest (see Tip, page 33)	**2 tsp.**	**10 mL**
Ground cinnamon	**1 tsp.**	**5 mL**
Dried cranberries	**1 cup**	**250 mL**
Salted, roasted shelled pumpkin seeds	**1 cup**	**250 mL**
Salted, roasted sunflower seeds	**1/2 cup**	**125 mL**

Process almonds in food processor until finely ground. Add dates and apricots. Process until fruit is finely chopped.

Add next 4 ingredients. Process until combined. Transfer to large bowl.

Add remaining 3 ingredients. Mix well to combine. Press firmly into greased parchment paper–lined 9 x 9 inch (23 x 23 cm) pan. Chill, covered, overnight. Remove from pan. Cuts into 24 bars.

1 bar: *200 Calories; 11 g Total Fat (4 g Mono, 2.5 g Poly, 1 g Sat); 0 mg Cholesterol; 23 g Carbohydrate; 4 g Fibre; 6 g Protein; 15 mg Sodium*

tip To toast nuts, seeds or coconut, place them in an ungreased frying pan. Heat on medium for 3 to 5 minutes, stirring often, until golden. To bake, spread them evenly in an ungreased shallow pan. Bake in a 350°F (175°C) oven for 5 to 10 minutes, stirring or shaking often, until golden.

Apple Nut Roll-ups

Crisp cinnamon-sugared tortilla spirals filled with apple, cranberries and coconut. These make a great snack and they're also sweet enough for dessert.

Finely chopped pecans, toasted (see Tip, page 148)	**1/2 cup**	**125 mL**
Grated unpeeled tart apple (such as Granny Smith)	**1/2 cup**	**125 mL**
Medium sweetened coconut, toasted	**1/2 cup**	**125 mL**
Almond butter	**1/3 cup**	**75 mL**
Flour tortillas (9 inch, 23 cm, diameter)	**2**	**2**
Finely diced unpeeled tart apple (such as Granny Smith)	**3/4 cup**	**175 mL**
Chopped dried cranberries	**1/3 cup**	**75 mL**
Cooking spray		
Granulated sugar	**2 tbsp.**	**30 mL**
Ground cinnamon	**1 tsp.**	**5 mL**

Combine first 4 ingredients in small bowl.

Spread on flour tortillas, leaving 1/2 inch (12 mm) edge. Scatter second amount of apple and cranberries over nut mixture. Fold sides over filling. Roll up tightly from bottom. Secure with wooden picks.

Spray rolls with cooking spray. Combine sugar and cinnamon in shallow dish. Roll tortillas in sugar mixture. Spray with cooking spray. Arrange on greased baking sheet. Bake in 450°F (230°C) oven for about 10 minutes until golden and crisp. Let stand for 5 minutes. Trim ends. Cuts into 8 pieces each. Makes 16 roll-ups.

***1 roll-up:** 120 Calories; 7 g Total Fat (2 g Mono, 1 g Poly, 1.5 g Sat); 0 mg Cholesterol; 13 g Carbohydrate; 2 g Fibre; 3 g Protein; 55 mg Sodium*

Pictured on page 90.

Lemon Coconut Cupcakes

Tender cupcakes that are perfectly accented by bright lemon notes and a light icing glaze. A perfect sweet for those with egg or dairy allergies—or for almost anyone, for that matter!

All-purpose flour	**1 3/4 cups**	**425 mL**
Granulated sugar	**1 cup**	**250 mL**
Baking powder	**2 tsp.**	**10 mL**
Baking soda	**1/2 tsp.**	**2 mL**
Salt	**1/4 tsp.**	**1 mL**
Soy milk	**1 1/4 cups**	**300 mL**
Cooking oil	**1/3 cup**	**75 mL**
Lemon juice	**1 tbsp.**	**15 mL**
Vanilla extract	**2 tsp.**	**10 mL**
Grated lemon zest (see Tip, page 33)	**1 tsp.**	**5 mL**
Icing (confectioner's) sugar	**2 cups**	**500 mL**
Lemon juice	**3 tbsp.**	**45 mL**
Shredded coconut, toasted (see Tip, page 148)	**1/4 cup**	**60 mL**

Combine first 5 ingredients in large bowl. Make a well in centre.

Whisk next 5 ingredients in small bowl. Add to well. Stir until smooth. Fill 12 paper-lined muffin cups 3/4 full. Bake in 350°F (175°C) oven for about 20 minutes until wooden pick inserted in centre of cupcake comes out clean. Let stand in pan for 5 minutes before removing to wire rack to cool completely.

Beat icing sugar and lemon juice in medium bowl until smooth. Spread on cupcakes.

Sprinkle with coconut. Makes 12 cupcakes.

1 cupcake: *270 Calories; 7 g Total Fat (4 g Mono, 2 g Poly, 1 g Sat); 0 mg Cholesterol; 50 g Carbohydrate; trace Fibre; 3 g Protein; 170 mg Sodium*

Pictured on page 90.

Chocolate Banana Almond Ice Cream

Bananas give this dark-coloured chocolate ice cream a smooth, creamy texture. Let it stand at room temperature for a few minutes so that it will scoop easily. For a vegan version, use chocolate that doesn't contain dairy products. Garnish with banana chips.

Unsweetened chocolate baking squares (1 oz., 28 g, each), chopped	**4**	**4**
Ripe medium bananas, cut up	**3**	**3**
Vanilla soy (or rice) milk	**1 1/2 cups**	**375 mL**
Almond butter	**1/2 cup**	**125 mL**
White corn syrup	**6 tbsp.**	**90 mL**
Brown sugar, packed	**1/4 cup**	**60 mL**

Put chocolate in small microwave-safe bowl. Microwave on medium (50%) for about 90 seconds, stirring every 30 seconds, until almost melted (see Tip, page 133). Stir until smooth. Transfer to blender.

Add remaining 5 ingredients. Process until smooth. Transfer to ungreased 9 x 9 inch (23 x 23 cm) pan. Freeze for about 2 hours until set. Makes about 4 1/2 cups (1.1 L).

1/2 cup (125 mL): *260 Calories; 15 g Total Fat (0 g Mono, 0 g Poly, 4.5 g Sat); 0 mg Cholesterol; 33 g Carbohydrate; 4 g Fibre; 6 g Protein; 35 mg Sodium*

Pictured on page 126.

Measurement Tables

Throughout this book measurements are given in Conventional and Metric measure. To compensate for differences between the two measurements due to rounding, a full metric measure is not always used. The cup used is the standard 8 fluid ounce. Temperature is given in degrees Fahrenheit and Celsius. Baking pan measurements are in inches and centimetres as well as quarts and litres. An exact metric conversion is given below as well as the working equivalent (Metric Standard Measure).

Spoons

Conventional Measure	Metric Exact Conversion Millilitre (mL)	Metric Standard Measure Millilitre (mL)
1/8 teaspoon (tsp.)	0.6 mL	0.5 mL
1/4 teaspoon (tsp.)	1.2 mL	1 mL
1/2 teaspoon (tsp.)	2.4 mL	2 mL
1 teaspoon (tsp.)	4.7 mL	5 mL
2 teaspoons (tsp.)	9.4 mL	10 mL
1 tablespoon (tbsp.)	14.2 mL	15 mL

Oven Temperatures

Fahrenheit (°F)	Celsius (°C)
175°	80°
200°	95°
225°	110°
250°	120°
275°	140°
300°	150°
325°	160°
350°	175°
375°	190°
400°	205°
425°	220°
450°	230°
475°	240°
500°	260°

Pans

Conventional Inches	Metric Centimetres
8x8 inch	20x20 cm
9x9 inch	23x23 cm
9x13 inch	23x33 cm
10x15 inch	25x38 cm
11x17 inch	28x43 cm
8x2 inch round	20x5 cm
9x2 inch round	23x5 cm
10x4 1/2 inch tube	25x11 cm
8x4x3 inch loaf	20x10x7.5 cm
9x5x3 inch loaf	23x12.5x7.5 cm

Cups

Conventional Measure	Metric Exact Conversion Millilitre (mL)	Metric Standard Measure Millilitre (mL)
1/4 cup (4 tbsp.)	56.8 mL	60 mL
1/3 cup (5 1/3 tbsp.)	75.6 mL	75 mL
1/2 cup (8 tbsp.)	113.7 mL	125 mL
2/3 cup (10 2/3 tbsp.)	151.2 mL	150 mL
3/4 cup (12 tbsp.)	170.5 mL	175 mL
1 cup (16 tbsp.)	227.3 mL	250 mL
4 1/2 cups	1022.9 mL	1000 mL (1 L)

Dry Measurements

Conventional Measure Ounces (oz.)	Metric Exact Conversion Grams (g)	Metric Standard Measure Grams (g)
1 oz.	28.3 g	28 g
2 oz.	56.7 g	57 g
3 oz.	85.0 g	85 g
4 oz.	113.4 g	125 g
5 oz.	141.7 g	140 g
6 oz.	170.1 g	170 g
7 oz.	198.4 g	200 g
8 oz.	226.8 g	250 g
16 oz.	453.6 g	500 g
32 oz.	907.2 g	1000 g (1 kg)

Casseroles

CANADA & BRITAIN		UNITED STATES	
Standard Size Casserole	Exact Metric Measure	Standard Size Casserole	Exact Metric Measure
1 qt. (5 cups)	1.13 L	1 qt. (4 cups)	900 mL
1 1/2 qts. (7 1/2 cups)	1.69 L	1 1/2 qts. (6 cups)	1.35 L
2 qts. (10 cups)	2.25 L	2 qts. (8 cups)	1.8 L
2 1/2 qts. (12 1/2 cups)	2.81 L	2 1/2 qts. (10 cups)	2.25 L
3 qts. (15 cups)	3.38 L	3 qts. (12 cups)	2.7 L
4 qts. (20 cups)	4.5 L	4 qts. (16 cups)	3.6 L
5 qts. (25 cups)	5.63 L	5 qts. (20 cups)	4.5 L

Recipe Index

A

B

C

D

Q

R

S

T

V

W

Z